UNFOLDING THE UNEXPECTEDNESS OF UNCERTAINTY

Social Fictions Series

Series Editor
Patricia Leavy
USA

The *Social Fictions* series emerges out of the arts-based research movement. The series includes full-length fiction books that are informed by social research but written in a literary/artistic form (novels, plays, and short story collections). Believing there is much to learn through fiction, the series only includes works written entirely in the literary medium adapted. Each book includes an academic introduction that explains the research and teaching that informs the book as well as how the book can be used in college courses. The books are underscored with social science or other scholarly perspectives and intended to be relevant to the lives of college students—to tap into important issues in the unique ways that artistic or literary forms can.

Please email queries to pleavy7@aol.com

Unfolding the Unexpectedness of Uncertainty

Creative Nonfiction and the Lives of Becoming Teachers

By

Anita Sinner
Concordia University, Montreal, Canada

SENSE PUBLISHERS
ROTTERDAM / BOSTON / TAIPEI

A C.I.P. record for this book is available from the Library of Congress.

ISBN 978-94-6209-354-6 (paperback)
ISBN 978-94-6209-355-3 (hardback)
ISBN 978-94-6209-356-0 (e-book)

Published by: Sense Publishers,
P.O. Box 21858, 3001 AW Rotterdam, The Netherlands
https://www.sensepublishers.com/

Cover art by Ruth, Ann and Nathalie.

Printed on acid-free paper

DEDICATION

This book is dedicated to the storytellers in my life:

To Mike, for all the years of laughter;
To Renate and Joseph, for making the past real;
To Chris, for always crafting a good tale;
To Sylvia, for the imaginative possibilities.

Thank you for inspiring my journey.

TABLE OF CONTENTS

CONTENTS

ACKNOWLEDGEMENTS

To Ruth, Ann and Nathalie, our teachers of tomorrow, I salute you.

I would like to extend my heartfelt appreciation to Carl Leggo and Erika Hasebe-Ludt, dear mentors and friends, for their commitment to the importance of stories, and to Patricia Leavy for her vision to make this book series possible.

I wish to express my gratitude to the Social Sciences and Humanities Research Council of Canada for support of this research.

Some of this book has been reprinted with permission from previously published articles in the following peer-reviewed journals:

Sinner, A. (2012). A game of dramatic hats: A counter-narrative in teacher education. *Teachers & Teaching: Theory & Practice, 18*(5), 601-613.

Sinner, A. (2010). Negotiating spaces: The in-betweenness of becoming a teacher. *Asia-Pacific Journal of Teacher Education, 38*(1), 23-37.

Sinner, A. (2010). Arts research as a triptych installation: A framework for interpreting and rendering enquiry. *International Journal of Education through Art, 6*(2), 125-142.

FOREWORD

WONDERING ALOUD & WANDERING ALLOWED

Ten Gestures Toward a Foreword

Carl Leggo
University of British Columbia

1

While reading Anita Sinner's *Unfolding the Unexpectedness of Uncertainty*, I often felt like I was viewing a documentary of beginning teachers' stories that were familiar, even haunting. I have been in school all my life. At fifty-nine years old, I definitely feel old (practically worn out), but with age I also feel a measure of sagacity. My wife Lana (who has loved me a very long time) gladly notes my sage age. Perhaps I am like an aged whiskey or a leather jacket that has worn into a supple, sturdy comfort. The stories of Ruth, Ann and Nathalie remind me that I was once young, once at the beginning of a teaching career. Reading their stories, I resonate with each of them, with their joys, hopes, fears, and frustrations. And, above all, I remember my stories. When we tell stories, we learn to lean on one another, learn to lean into the lines that support, even suspend us like braided ropes that help us walk in the heart's light.

2

Like all her artistic and scholarly and pedagogical convictions, Anita is committed to creative nonfiction as a way of inquiring and knowing because creative nonfiction is located in the stories of daily experience, rendered with thoughtful care for aesthetics and ethics. I have known Anita a long time. She is a constant blessing in my life, a companion who has walked with me in many journeys. The lovely word *companion* is etymologically connected to the Latin *cum pane* or *with bread*. We have enjoyed bread together (never more than in Montreal with a legendary smoked meat sandwich). Actually, we have worked so closely together, it is like we have made bread together, kneaded the dough, sprinkled in the yeast, waited for it to bake. And how appropriate it is to reflect on the action of *making* and *kneading*. The word *fiction* is derived from a Latin word *fingere, to make or to form*, even like kneading and shaping clay or dough to create something new. Anita is an extraordinary artist and researcher and teacher who calls together stories and renders them with careful creativity so others can hear the lyrical rhythms of the heart in all our stories.

3

In some ways creative nonfiction might seem like an oxymoron or a redundant phrase. Isn't all writing creative? Isn't all writing fiction? Isn't nonfiction really another fiction clinging to contested claims of reality? These are questions I have lingered with a long time, and I anticipate that I will continue to linger much longer. Anita promotes creative nonfiction because she loves people. Integral to all Anita's research is inviting, encouraging, and sustaining the voices of others, especially the voices of others who can be too easily forgotten or ignored, others who have been silenced. So, while I can argue about the etymology and experience of fiction, I happily acknowledge how Anita uses creative nonfiction in order to promote research and writing that are rooted in the earth, the humus that connects all of us in an inextricable tangle of stories that know no beginning and ending. Our stories begin with etcetera, and they end with etcetera.

4

Anita lives in the fecund possibilities of prefixes. She does not attempt to fix anything. In *Unfolding the Unexpectedness of Uncertainty*, Anita lingers with the prefix *un*, the most prolific prefix in English, because *un* does not only denote negation—it also connotes otherness and difference. To add *un* to a word is to turn the original word with a sharp twist that compels us to see the original word anew, with startled eyes, with possibilities for wonder.

5

Anita, Nathalie, Ann, and Ruth remind us that story is a way (if I were bolder, I might write *the way*, but I am always concerned about fundamentalist claims that leave no room for fun) for understanding our world, for standing in words in the world, for standing in relationship to one another with prepositional possibilities beyond counting. As human beings we are human be-com-ings. By wondering and wandering in stories, we *become*, uniquely and idiosyncratically, communally and corporately.

6

What I enjoy most in the stories of Ann, Ruth, and Nathalie is how they acknowledge, even embrace, uncertainty. So much curriculum and pedagogy has been constructed and constrained in a relentlessly rigorous march to the place of certainty where discernment is no longer needed because everything we need to know is already known. If we can just determine how the brain functions and how learners learn, then we can determine how to organize effective and efficient education. If we can determine how to manage both rule-constrained and unruly students and how to evaluate their learning and how to decide what is important to know and what is less important, then we can organize schooling and teacher education and art education. Of course, in the course of all that efficient organization, we will have missed how education is wandering and wondering in uncertainty, in mystery, in the volcanic and vorticular heart of the whirling world we hardly know.

7

As Ruth, Ann and Nathalie unfold their experiences, they compose other folds. Like a North Atlantic wind in January will shape snow in an always mutable chaos with only a tentative cosmos, Ann, Ruth, and Nathalie know their stories are always changing, always wandering full of wonder. Nathalie, Ann, and Ruth are negotiating emergent identities as teachers, holding fast to the past identities of artists, wondering if these identities, named separately, will find interstices of dynamic connection or will find the chasm that renders chaos so chronically fearful. And, happily, by navigating the twists and turns, the detours and diversions, of their year in teacher education, they find their stories constructed in the crosswise arrangement of chiasmus where every step forward is repeated in reverse order, so teacher education is about teaching teachers as well as teachers teaching, always becoming.

8

Art is prophetic and passionate. Art infuses the art educator's spirit with a precarious poise and a capacious conviction for living into the pedagogy of (im)possibility. Art educators learn to live their curriculum. They learn to become their curriculum.

9

Unfolding the Unexpectedness of Uncertainty folds and unfolds the unexpectedness of uncertainty, the expectedness of uncertainty, the unexpectedness of certainty, and the expectedness of certainty, so the only certainty is uncertainty, and the only expectedness is unexpectedness. In the end, as in the beginning, the teacher wanders and wonders, creating stories with attention and intention. And with those stories, teacher initiation, teacher identity, and teacher inquiry are all expanded and transformed as experiences are narrated from inside the classrooms, the imaginations, the hearts of artists who are becoming teachers, fired by the arts to create new possibilities for teaching and learning.

10

As a poet I like to leave poems, seldom sure anyone will want to attend to them. I offer the poems in a kind of silent benediction, an offering that expects no reciprocity, an offering of hope for words and creativity and stories and communication, invitations for communion, love notes because the heart is called to the art of pedagogy, filled with love. So, I conclude these gestures toward a foreword with a poem about growing old, recognizing joy, and becoming ....

Smiley

at fifty-nine
I have finally
      caught up
with the smiling face
of the 70s iconic,
      perhaps ironic,
certainly ubiquitous
wide-eyed Greek
comic mask, once
long ago, pinned
to my bedroom wall

the mask first born
in 1953, my year too

I am happy
      I am having a nice day

when young,
Lana asked me
      often
if I would ever
be happy

      after years
of grumpy responses
she stopped asking

now I am old
with enough aches
& brokenness
to remind me
          constantly
my biological
& chronological
          sixty is just
around the corner

& knowing so
many who had
          no chance
to turn the corner

I am happy
          I am having a nice day

like a tightrope walk
on the braided threads
of the heart's light
I walk the curriculum
          of delight
with a precarious poise
between emotions
          & emoticons
Forrest Gump's muddy face
& Wal-Mart's sales job

conscious
          conscientious
even conscientized

still unfolding
          the unexpectedness
          of uncertainty
in stories shaped

in the lines of lives
becoming teachers

Thank you, Ruth, Ann and Nathalie, for your stories, full of hope and conviction, and thank you, Anita, for your commitment to hearing the heart of others' stories and rendering the stories with artful care so we know ourselves in relationship and in process.

CREATIVE NONFICTION AS A METHOD OF INQUIRY

As an expression of arts research, this book explores the lived experiences of three women, Ruth, Ann and Nathalie (pseudonyms), as they became art teachers over the course of their certification year. Rendering their experiences as short stories from the field of teacher education brings a social research dimension to scholarship through the literary form of creative nonfiction, in which stories act as catalysts to understand teacher culture from first-person accounts (Ellis, 2002; Richardson, 1994).

I engage Ruth, Ann and Nathalie as research partners, not participants, during this journey. Their stories may be described as openings: Ruth's unfolding; Ann's unexpectedness; and Nathalie's uncertainty. It is my intention that their stories stand as exemplars of arts research, and as an invitation to readers to consider multiple readings, understandings and writings of these narratives rather than closing stories to static interpretations. By attending to social biography in ways that extend the purpose, intent, outcomes and dissemination of research, these stories serve as a means to express and make accessible scholarly study that invites a more intimate connectivity to students becoming teachers and to teacher educators. This scholarly work also expands Genette's (1997) conceptualisation of the *ébauche,* or underpainting of research, by demonstrating two core commitments to readers of this book. Firstly, these stories bring forward transdisciplinary openings (Leavy, 2011) for undergraduate and graduate students and academic researchers in fields of study involving creative nonfiction and life writing, with primary interest in Education, Creative Writing, English, Women's Studies, Social and Cultural Geography, Sociology and Integrated Studies. Secondly, these stories are collectively offered as exemplars of customary methodological practices that are part of shifting *post-post* paradigms already underway, making the medium of stories a resource for scholars interested in exploring arts research methods in the academy today.

Written in accessible language, this book invites a broad readership by documenting and describing the lived experiences of students entering a professional practice. In this way, this book offers educative value to schools and community-based educators, policy-makers, curriculum designers and researchers as well as audiences beyond the academy.

Creative nonfiction as arts research

Creative nonfiction is a hybrid approach that is somewhat controversial in the academy, blurring traditional methods of dissemination in an effort to better communicate the educational significance of research. The application of the literary form of creative nonfiction, which renders facts and events (content) with the conventions of fiction writing (form) – including narrative voice, persona, authentic characterisation of place and settings, and pursuit of an idea or goal – is an emerging genre of life writing in both qualitative and arts research discourses (Hasebe-Ludt, 2010). Creative nonfiction begins with transdisciplinary perspectives on the constructs and practices of expressing self in a broader social community, and it is within this conversation that I enter each story. According to Leggo (2008), through the "principal dynamics" of storying (what happened), discourse (the form and construction of the story) and interpretation (how the story is understood), "fragments of experience" are shaped in ways that "remind us that there is significance in the moment, in the particular, in the mundane" (pp. 3, 7). In this case, the narrative development was, as Britzman (2007) suggests, "uneven" and at times "out of joint," which was "made stranger by the postmodern university where teacher education occurs" (p. 1). Storying experience focuses on layers within the social geography of teacher education that attend to "moral" dimensions of teaching, and make becoming a teacher more "visible" (Estola, 2003, p. 182). Creative nonfiction thus provides a medium and method through which to reveal practices within the current situation of teacher education, and at the same time provides a means to push the boundaries of the profession. For Ruth, Ann and

Nathalie, the transformative process of becoming a teacher required a continual reinterpreting of self in relation to teacher culture, and through the development of narratives, their stories open spaces that may have otherwise remained hidden or unrecognised. According to Tilden (2004), creative nonfiction is "grounded in the profusion of everyday life" and it is always "written against loss" where stories are "eccentric and centric...in the sense of deviation from the expected, the idealised master-story – and also in the sense of generation from and reference to a common cultural place" (pp. 708, 709). My approach echoes distinctive perspectives (Richardson, 2000), critical storytelling (Barone, 2000), and narrative experiments (Gough, 2003), all innovative modes of inquiry that bring creative forms of writing to educational studies, extending life writing as both a literary genre and a method of inquiry (Hasebe-Ludt, Chambers & Leggo, 2009).

Creative nonfiction invites debate about how becoming teachers write their own life stories as a means to actively inform professional development and program delivery. Entering research practices with a perspective that stories are effective teaching tools that represent cultural artefacts, I regard creative nonfiction as an artful way of knowing, moving understandings from identifying research partners objectively as students to more caring and subjective identification as individuals experiencing a series of momentous, life-changing events (Witherell & Noddings, 1991). Stories begin with personal experiences, where emotions are entry points to discerning the meaning of encounters reported by Ruth, Ann and Nathalie. Such storytelling requires trustworthy characters establishing distinct points of view that appeal to the reader's emotions in an effort to make sense of experiences in public schools as student-teachers and in postsecondary teacher training. By engaging with their lived experiences, I considered how their stories rupture research in ways that traditional approaches might not, and how through such expression, social research illuminates aspects of becoming a teacher that generate the power of that moment in their lives. Because pre-service teachers move through multiple learning communities during teacher education programs, they emerged as authentic insiders, sharing situated knowledge to guide the future of teacher education by drawing attention to internal shifts underway in professional practice. It is incumbent on researchers concerned with the nature of teaching to listen to and respond to those who are living the experience to ensure the profession and the field of study remain robust. Although pre-service teacher education is a well-established area of study with a host of themes defining inquiry, creative nonfiction draws attention to the tensions, challenges and in-betweenness that emerge when negotiating new definitions of self within the constructs in teacher education.

Establishing storytelling as a method of inquiry that does not conform to dominant theories or genres creates conditions to reconsider, rethink and redefine how information is understood and what knowing should be at the forefront in scholarship as a means to move toward greater social, political and intellectual consciousness. It may be argued too that employing creative nonfiction as a researcher involves risk-taking, for as Sachs (2010) suggests, when "writing against the formula" of the academic "fetishization" of objectivity, there is often a "wait until tenure" approach "to write the way we want to" (p. 7). I appreciate alternate methodologies and methods like creative nonfiction attract advocates and critics, and I am left reflecting on the importance of disseminating such work as research, given entrenched locations of power within the academy. I am reminded of Lynn Raphael Reed's writing: "I can feel the gaze of authoritative discourse on my shoulder in disapproval of the venture, and I am reminded to be cautious about revelation" (Reed in Francis & Skelton, 2001, p. 79). In turn, Gallagher (2011) argues that "storytelling is centrally important to educational research," bringing "a partial and intersubjective critical experience" forward as students seek a sense of belonging to the teaching profession (p. 49). Mindful of these considerations, I realized early on that this study required my engagement in literary arts to understand the lived experiences of visual art students. At the outset it was clear Ruth, Ann and Nathalie were actively storying experience through a variety of artful mediums available to them. So extensive was the act of storying, I felt remiss to impose my research leanings onto this study, and instead followed the lead of my partners to customize my approach accordingly. Adopting a literary perspective, I immersed myself in the practices of writing, experimenting with different modes of expression. Yet in creating narratives of becoming, I followed a process similar to visual composition: selecting a series of elements in particular ways to convey meaning-making to an audience. Stories were composed collaboratively by blending elements of conversations, emails, reflections, as well as hundreds of pages of transcripts from over fifty interviews and a significant archive of artworks they had produced during their teacher education program. From multiple sources, words were copied verbatim to retain each partner's voice in a process of selecting experiences that resonated most strongly for them. By investigating and documenting creative nonfiction as life writing, and exploring the significance of this approach for teacher educators, teacher stories double as a pedagogic act and as intertexts of identity and place (Barthes, 1977; Gough, 1994; Chambers, Hasebe-Ludt, Leggo & Sinner, 2012). In this way, I recognize creative nonfiction is a responsive and fluid literary genre where the contexts of everyday stories are not singular events but a form of relational interactivity, thereby affirming that storying has a critical role to perform in conveying intimate understandings of the lived experiences of teachers and at the same time serves as a forum for learning about becoming a teacher. This research framework extends to how creative nonfiction emerges as a medium that renders stories and accommodates and inspires diverse ways of thinking about experience.

By mapping convergences between expressive language, research and the educational landscape, knowledge construction through creative nonfiction was a collective process between me and Ruth, Ann and Nathalie. As an arts researcher, my goal is to embrace the particularities of lived experiences that are evident through storying self, and our one-to-one meetings that began in early September set the tone for our evolving research relationships. I encouraged free interaction as a practice during the interviews, which generated what I describe as synergistic bonding in our conversations. I invited collaboration on every aspect, including selecting questions, transcript reviews and member checks of the written report. As partners they were encouraged to take control of segments of the writing, to remove any passages they felt were too revealing or too personal. As a researcher, I sought to "avoid control" and to develop "a sense of connectedness" with partners in an "atmosphere in which women felt knowledgeable" (Reinharz, 1992, pp. 20, 25). I wanted partners to tell their stories their own way, so we met frequently in person, engaged in extensive dialogue and built solid working research relationships that sustained the project over a year, resulting in the quality, type and scope of information that informs this study.

In practice this was reinforced in everyday actions, for example, we routinely met in an available office, sometimes a classroom or a café. We shared tea, coffee and snacks, attending to our comfort during our conversations. Our meetings were social encounters, planned for an hour, but frequently extending to two or three hours. We spoke with great ease, and as an active listener I reciprocated, sharing my personal experiences in self-disclosure. Yet sometimes during our conversations I wondered, could I really gauge how they felt in a particular moment in time?

I was equally conscious that my decisions and actions in the course of our meetings were consequential. From the outset I transcribed our audio-recorded conversations, and sent transcripts to the individual partners for review in a process which continued until the completion of the study. Transcribing our conversations was exhaustive but vital in analysing data while collecting data. The experience of transcribing allowed me to relive the conversations, to hear specificities in life stories and segues of experiences that were emerging in varied forms but linking together across conversational time. The more I listened while writing out their words, the more linkages were lifting out of the transcripts and registering in my understanding of their becoming, both as particular and general themes within their evolving stories. Such revelations would not have happened for me if I had relinquished transcriptions to a third party. I learn by doing, and the hands-on laborious task of transcription was central in my coming to know.

It was clear throughout the year that the women were most interested in talking about issues relating to the experience of becoming an art teacher. They were already teaching me about becoming from an expert position, disclosing meaning-making regarding their journey in ways I could not have anticipated or been sensitive to had I undertaken another research design. It was my duty as a researcher to discover what they knew to be of value. My partners were active agents in shaping how their stories operated as sites of negotiation for their emerging teacher identities. I quickly became absorbed in the stories, and I continued to think with and in their stories of becoming, a process through which I unveiled my own subjectivity (Pillow, 2003). With this holistic approach to research, we came to operate on multiple levels: as friends, peers, mentors and learners. The unfolding of research is a story of success and frustration, of hopes and dreams, for participants as partners and for me as researcher.

I came to adopt the axiological position that these textual expressions were gestures (Genette, 1997, p. 143). As gestures, such expressions primarily represent a way to communicate experience through storytelling. Making space for stories in research enlarges notions of arts research in constructive and educational ways, and shifts the focus of discussion from *what* (types of artistic function) to *when* (how art operates within research) (Genette 1997). This process places less emphasis on the art genre and more on the aesthetic function and effects of doing research through the arts. In this way, the literary arts provide a framework for an organic approach to research that is concerned with *when* is art, and implies that works of creative nonfiction in research are part of the larger arts paradigm that requires a conceptual understanding of artistic and aesthetic characteristics (Genette 1999). For as Spindler (2008) advocates, "informed criticism as an alternative to pre-determined criteria" is a means to rigorously and vigorously judge stories "that open writerly texts" in academic contexts and transform professional practice, something Ruth, Ann and Nathalie were keenly aware of doing through storying critical events (p. 19).

These research decisions and realizations incur ethical responsibilities, and as an arts researcher, I have an obligation to engage in research in ways that best enriches educational discourse. From a perspective that all research is partial, the challenge then is to take up data collection through interviews from a methodological disposition of deep listening, making the writing of the story a process, practice and product of rhetorical and metaphorical knowing that brings Ruth, Ann and Nathalie into research with a subjective presence. In this book, research partners each offer their stories as a means to deliver detailed and often evocative information about becoming a teacher, resulting in compelling stories with rich, creative and intellectual qualities required of academic scholarship. The stories that follow demonstrate pedagogic understandings and have curricular implications for teaching a new generation of learners from experiential and aesthetic perspectives. In each case, the scene is framed with theoretical and methodological stances that remain implicit in the background, revealing the power of story in research and the potential to locate self in stories to provoke more questions, focus attention on the gaps within teacher education, and grant insight to moments of conjunction, disjunction and even trauma that informs identity construction for students becoming teachers. Much like Santos (2012), through storytelling I do not seek consensus, but look to engage the audience to think about the scope of teacher education "while visiting different perspectives" in which "making public is its validation," for "the more perspectives I consider when I tell a story, the more impartial my story can become" (pp. 113, 116).

Despite extensive inquiry into dimensions of teacher education, there remains surprisingly little research that examines teacher culture from first-person accounts. To date, this lack of research addressing how the stories of teaching and teachers are conceptualized, created, distributed and assessed suggests a gap exists within the field of study. There are no extensive resources about the impact of working in a profession that fails to situate the lives of teachers in the history of education; nor are there general practices within education institutions to integrate the lived experiences of students becoming teachers as a means to improve practices. Recognising the pedagogic role of a teacher is always evolving, this book initiates a discussion of dispositions by adopting creative nonfiction to attend to an area of study that has not been adequately documented or problematised in the research literature. Through creative nonfiction, I suggest that teacher education becomes an expansive educational space that further shifts our understandings of knowledge creation. Stories encourage teachers to express a creative and critical voice to contribute to the changing socio-cultural fabric of the profession. With respect to our increasingly transdisciplinary practices, it is our responsibility as researchers to initiate, negotiate and actively participate in the development of institutional structures that recognize the value of real life accounts of teachers. In so doing, teacher education will become a more responsive practice with narratives about teachers, for teachers, by teachers.

Stories told by student-teachers serve as a means to create relationships within research that offer portrayals of experience which move beyond traditional data analysis of telling research to showing research. I propose that employing technical devices of tone, plotlines, tension, setting the scene, as well as adopting colloquial expressions, reflective commentary and more, generates a more authentic rendering of teacher education, resonating with audiences through persuasive testimonies. Stories represented through creative nonfiction offer an alternate perspective to envision changing relationships between pre-service teachers and teaching culture. Creative nonfiction draws attention to the deeply intimate moments of becoming a teacher in an effort to better understand how to educate future teachers, and in this case, how to teach art and how to make art a means to enhance understandings of self. Such standpoints begin with a mindset of embracing an insider's point of view in relation to social constructions of individual narratives. Within this book, stories demonstrate aspects of convergence, as well as messy texts, to reveal the ethics of the spoken and written word at the heart of life writing (Hasebe-Ludt, Chambers & Leggo, 2009). As the researcher, I remain keenly aware of my own social influence in the course of developing these stories, and how my encounters with Ruth, Ann and Nathalie and their vulnerabilities as student-teachers were an ongoing negotiation of "beliefs, values and their inevitable conflicts in the classroom," while I strove to bring transparency to the research processes, practices and resulting products by asking, "what and how do we know?" (Allen, 2008, pp. 889, 897).

Creative nonfiction has the potential to change structures of learning and teaching, and in the process, provide a suitable method to write contemporary teacher stories. In this way, creative nonfiction as life writing represents a cornerstone of how parameters are changing for students becoming teachers, and how as researchers, we may conduct research and represent the impact of research through stories in the academy today.

REFERENCES

Allen, S. (2008). Reading the other: Ethics of encounter. *Educational Philosophy and Theory, 40*(7), 888-899.

Barone, T. (2000). *Aesthetics, politics and educational inquiry.* New York: Peter Lang.

Barthes, R. (1977). *Roland Barthes.* (R. Howard, Trans.). Berkeley: University of California Press.

Britzman, D. (2007). Teacher education as uneven development: Toward a psychology of uncertainty. *International Journal of Leadership in Education, 10*(1), 1-12.

Chambers, C., Hasebe-Ludt, E., & Leggo, C. (Eds.). (2012). *A heart of wisdom: Life writing as empathetic inquiry.* New York: Peter Lang.

Ellis, C. (2002). Being real: Moving inward toward social change. *Qualitative Studies in Education, 15*(4), 399-406.

Estola, E. (2003). Hope as work: Student teachers constructing their narrative identities. *Scandinavian Journal of Educational Research, 47*(2), 181-203.

Francis, B., & Skelton, C. (2001). *Investigating gender: Contemporary perspectives in education.* Buckingham, England: Open University Press.

Gallagher, K. (2011). In search of a theoretical basis for storytelling in education research: Story as method. *International Journal of Research and Method, 34*(1), 49-61.

Genette, G. (1997). *The work of art: Immanence and transcendence* (G. M. Goshgarian, Trans.). Ithaca, NY: Cornell University Press.

Genette, G. (1999). *The aesthetic relation* (G. M. Goshgarian, Trans.). Ithaca, New York: Cornell University Press.

Gough, N. (2003). *Intertextual turns in curriculum inquiry: Fictions, diffractions and deconstructions.* Unpublished doctoral dissertation, University of Deakin, Australia.

Gough, N. (2004). Read intertextually, write an essay, make a rhizome: Performing narrative experiments in educational inquiry. In H. Piper & I. Stronach (Eds.), *Educational research: Difference and diversity* (pp. 155-176). Aldershot, UK: Ashgate.

Hasebe-Ludt, E. (2010). *Portrayals of teachers' lives: Investigating teacher education through popular culture and digital media as arts education.* Social Sciences and Humanities Standard Research Grant #410-2010-2192 (2010-2015). A. Sinner, Principal Investigator, Concordia University; Co-investigators: E. Hasebe-Ludt, University of Lethbridge; and C. Leggo, University of British Columbia.

Hasebe-Ludt, E., Chambers, C., & Leggo, C. (2009). *Life writing and literary métissage as an ethos for our times*. New York: Peter Lang.

Leavy, P. (2011). *Essentials of transdisciplinary research: Using problem-centred methodologies*. Walnut Creek, CA: Left Coast Press.

Leggo, C. (2008). Narrative inquiry: Attending to the art of discourse. *Language & Literacy, 10*, 1. Available at: http://www.langandlit.ualberta.ca/current.html

Pillow, W. (2003). Confession, catharsis, or cure? Rethinking the uses of reflexivity as methodological power in qualitative research. *Qualitative Studies in Education, 16*(2), 175-196.

Reinharz, S. (1992). *Feminist methods in social research*. New York: Oxford University Press.

Richardson, L. (1994). Writing: A method of inquiry. In N. K. Denzin & Y. Lincoln (Eds.), *Handbook of qualitative research* (pp. 516-529). Thousand Oaks, CA: Sage.

Richardson, L. (2000). Evaluating ethnography. *Qualitative Inquiry, 6*(2), 253-255.

Sachs, A. (2010). Letters to a tenured historian: Imagining history as creative nonfiction – or maybe even poetry. *Rethinking History, 14*(1), 5-38.

Santos, D. (2012). The politics of storytelling: Unfolding the multiple layers of politics in (P)AR publications. *Educational Action Research, 20*(1), 113-128.

Spindler, J. (2008). Fictional writing, educational research and professional learning. *International Journal of Research and Method in Education, 31*(1), 19-30.

Tilden, N. (2004). Nothing quite your own: Reflections on creative nonfiction. *Women's Studies, 33*, 707-718.

Witherell, C., & Noddings, N. (Eds.). (1991). *Stories lives tell: Narrative and dialogue in education*. New York: Teachers College Press.

UNFOLDING:
RUTH'S STORY

I'm going to build a bridge

I always wanted to be an art teacher. It started off because my mom wanted to be a teacher. She was a teacher's assistant and she worked with a lot of special needs kids. I have always been the one in my family to pick up the pencil and paper and draw, whether it be my favourite image, *Ariel the Little Mermaid,* or anything else. That was always me, and I think loving drawing, and watching my mom at work and hearing her stories came together and became a goal for me. It just always made sense to me that teaching is what I wanted to do. So I've never really looked away from this goal. I would never doubt that I'm supposed to be here.

I went from high school right into university and completed my arts degree with a major in fine arts and a minor in French. I don't really have any outside experience in terms of teaching a class. I've observed in classrooms of my own accord. I had a tough time deciding what grade level I wanted to teach, elementary or high school. In the end, I decided that high school is really where I wanted to be because that's where I can teach the kids the kinds of things I love to do. It is one thing to colour with crayons and have kids make abstract stuff and say "that's so cute" or "tell me about that," but I really want to go a lot deeper and work through difficult issues with teenagers. It's not that you're not influencing kids when you're in an elementary school, because you are a huge influence, but just in a different way. Being able to express yourself and everything that comes along with being a teenager and experiencing everything is where I want to be. Kids need good teachers to help them through their years of high school and that's what has brought me here.

Now I'm taking teacher education and I'm quite young still, so that is one concern of mine about teaching high school. I don't want to fit in too well with the high school kids. I will be teaching kids that are only five years younger. Other students in the cohort have had experience in different jobs, they've done some traveling, they've done different things and now they're coming back and they have the life experience. I don't have that kind of life experience so to speak, outside of school. So what if I teach Grade 8 and they are sassy, and what about those Grade 12's, they'll tower over me! How am I going to be able to keep the peace, have the classroom management and just be able to teach them what they need to know about art, and why art is relevant these days. I thought back to my high school years and the way my teachers taught me, and do I want to be that kind of teacher? How might I do that? What would I want to change? A lot of questions started to fill up and although I know that they will be answered, what do I do in the meantime? Even though there's still that deeper fear, it looks more realistic now. I can feel comfortable knowing I will be taught how to deal with everything that comes along, and how to deal with changes. So even if there is something I'm not sure of now, I will know how to do it by the end of this program.

Our first day was really great. There were so many readings in the first week. You've got to read article, article, article, chapter, chapter, chapter, reading response, reading response, and then visual journal. I want to do all the readings and I want to retain everything I can in the readings, but they are telling us, skim and scan. It isn't about understanding everything; it is just about having those ideas. You just want your brain to hold everything in, but then there's that point of saturation, in one ear out the other, so by the time we got to the end of the first week I just wanted to do it again, to start over.

In high school, I tried to fit in and not to be noticed. In Grade 11, I started dating my husband. He was involved in everything: student council, student action, Counter Attack, everything. It was good for his resume, and it was good for scholarships. He has a real 'get those marks' attitude, and I've always had a good grade average, so he was the one who really got me into being a part of organizations, and in turn made me realize it was really good to put yourself out there and that brought me out of my shell. When I was in high school, I didn't miss class unless I absolutely had to. I wasn't necessarily the most energetic student, like 'I know this, pick me, pick me,' but I was very attentive. I'm a real people pleaser so I don't want to ruffle any feathers. I don't like to give my own opinions a lot of the time, especially if they differ from somebody else. I usually change my opinions, and say, 'Well that makes sense too, maybe I'm wrong.' In high school, I did an art piece at graduation about me starting off to university, looking into the sunset with my arms extended. In it, I'm outside and I'm going to build a bridge, so that is my metaphor for becoming a teacher.

I am a very personal artist. During my undergrad, we had to think of the concepts. I like to paint things that make sense to me, but it might not make a lot of sense to my audience, so at this point I would not be a good gallery artist. I don't think people understood what I was trying to say in my undergrad years. I tried my hardest to fit the 'whole family personal thing' into conceptual art but it didn't work out well. I remember making one project which was about my father, he's a policeman, and I loved this project. I wanted to portray my dad as more than a policeman. It is not just the suit. So I painted a series of three and it was my dad in the police uniform on the job, he's a highway patrolman; there was another one with me and my sister and my mom in an intimate setting; and then there's a third one. It was a very personal piece for me because I see my dad as so much more than a policeman. We had our critique in the classroom and I saw how much an audience can dismantle and turn around what you want to say. There was one student who apparently did not see policemen as useful assets of society and interpreted it in such a negative way. Really, how can I say it, it really hit me personally, because my work is so personal. I realized I don't like critique. At that point, even though I wanted my art to be personal, I had a hard time describing my art. It's all about my own experiences, my imagination, how my life is. I think my perception is really going to change this year in terms of how my art looks, and as I think about the students and what I want them to do. It's really pushing my own boundaries of what art is and how you can express yourself.

As a teacher, I'm a little bit unsure of myself, mostly because I have such a smattering of knowledge in a lot of places and I don't realize that the students I'm teaching are not going to have any. In the future, once I know a little more about students and about being a facilitator or guide, I will help students come down the same path that I did, in whatever way they are going. I'll have a lot to offer them, a lot of energy to impart to them, to give them the reins and say, "Let's go, let's just have fun!"

I really do feel like a seed, being opened up and putting roots down and waiting to find the sun, and just grow up. I'm really excited about everything. Right now I'm going everywhere, my brain isn't stopping. Last night I dreamt I was teaching. Everything in my life is teaching, teaching, teaching, but the fear of failing is always there, like when you do something for the first time that other people do professionally. I think, 'Oh, did I get it? Will I get it?' We're doing lesson plans right now and I went to talk to the instructor today because I'm really confused. There's so many different lesson plans, all these different templates, and all the words are different but they all mean the same thing. I don't get it. Other people are writing within the hour allotted and I've written down ten things but I've completely missed the process. That was a real eye opener. I had question after question. I don't get it, why don't I get it. I know I'm going to succeed because everyone is there to help, so it is unnecessary fear.

I might teach things differently than how I was taught in school. So much of art class is about identity and trying to figure out who you are. Anything from body image to self-image to gender issues, then there's the social justice classroom and teaching diversity and I could do so much with that. It isn't about the process necessarily. It can be about context and personal issues, and it can be anything you want it to be. I want to further that goal. I want to be able to make art about anything that the students want to do. I want to help them get where they want to go because whatever they have in their mind to do is art to them. It doesn't have to be open to critics, so I think that's my biggest goal for this year.

We went on a field trip with the cohort where we were in the role of observers. I wasn't a student anymore and it was very weird, because you're very familiar with the role of a high school student and a university student. I'm used to listening to a lecture for an hour, but going in the classroom I wasn't made to sit, I was just listening. It wasn't about a lecture anymore. It was about getting the kids involved and then letting them do their own thing. I really felt between worlds almost. I wasn't quite a teacher, so I wasn't in charge and I certainly wasn't the student, but at the same time, I was young enough still that a lot of things they are interested in are interesting to me too. It was very easy, and surprising that I could go up to a table of Grade 8 boys and ask them how they're doing, and we got into a whole discussion about Nintendo. As a teacher, I was wondering, is this allowed? As a teacher, do kids talk to them about their everyday stuff? But I still wasn't one of the group. I was an outsider. I was like a teacher, an incoming source, so they were careful about what they said. We talked a little bit about hockey starting in a couple of weeks and they were excited about that. It was a very out of body experience because I was so many things at once. I actually found it easier to talk to the guys, who have always intimidated me, than the girls, especially the Grade 9's, oh, they're snotty! I figured, I'm a girl, so sisterhood, but it was just after lunch and they were chatting rather than doing their art. The funny thing was, the other student-teachers were able to talk to other groups that I wasn't able to talk to, so it was weird, the people who I felt more comfortable with and less comfortable with. I think back to my high school, the art room was always open and kids would eat in there, and I think that is what made our room such a great place because we could sit together and talk. It created a sense of community.

In our cohort, we are practicing dressing as an artist or art teacher at the moment and it is amazing how some people look so much like art teachers. Totally teacherish! I just love it. What should I wear? What's artsy? What does an art teacher look like? You can't wear your best dress. I braided my hair, but that made me look 15, so I would never braid my hair again. I wore some big dangling earrings and a wrap that my mom got from the Caribbean with tassels on it. I wore some blue dress slacks. I'm really concerned about how to dress. You are an art teacher but an art teacher dresses differently than a regular teacher. I don't remember my art teachers ever wearing suits. You don't do that because you are going to get messy. So my mom and me went shopping and found six blazers for the price of one, which is fabulous. They were all different colors and they are all artsy. One of them is an empire waist, it's my favourite. I've got to look young and fun, but I have to look professional, and there's a difference between old professional and stylish young professional. I can see what people wear, but I can't necessarily put it together. I get ideas from other people in the class, like one girl she wears the coolest necklaces, I just love them. I want them so badly! She wears them every day and so having a little bit of funky jewellery can mix up a more professional outfit. This is as important as lesson plans.

If you fail to plan, you plan to fail

I'm at a point now that I've gotten to so many other times in my life, and I've never actually taken the next step. There is a threshold between the really wanting to, and actually doing it, the thought and the action. I have a lot of thresholds with learning language, even though I have a French minor. Learning and speaking a language are two very different things. I can understand French very well. In my classes, I never spoke a word because it was the threshold. I was scared to be wrong. I was scared to have my grammar in the wrong positions or forgetting words or pronouncing things incorrectly. I got into French as an English student. I never went to Immersion. I love languages and I love French; it is a beautiful language. I wish I could speak it. I can speak in my head perfectly, so someone says something to me, I know exactly what to say in my head, but in class I rarely spoke. There was that fear. I had the opportunity to go to Québec, but in the end, because my husband and I got engaged and then the marriage thing, the whole planning, I had to say no. So there was another threshold that I really wanted to cross, but at the same time, it was kind of comforting that I could say no, because I didn't have to cross that bridge. So I'm at that point right now again. I really want to be a teacher. I'm really excited about being a teacher and I want to do it. I want to teach what I have been learning, but there's still that fear, the whole bridge thing that I have to walk over. You can't walk over it in steps almost, you are either doing it, or you're not. I mean, we teach one lesson at a time, but you're either the teacher or you are not. We'll be observed in the first week of the practicum, which is really good, and then we will teach one lesson a day. It is like I have to jump to the whole other side, which is really scary for me, so I'm excited and at the same time scared out of my mind. I thought countless times of my dad saying, 'If you fail to plan, you plan to fail.' This is a big one, now I hear his words in the back my head.

I really want to go on Monday to my practicum and get over the initial fear. I want to be in the back of that classroom to document everything that happens and every single thing the teacher does. I want to model action for action, word for word. Then really what I'm doing is putting everything that I've learned so far into perspective which I want so badly but that fear is kind of right there. I know how to write things down. I know how to write the lesson plan. I know how to do the research because I learned that from my undergrad. I could have all of the information but it is the presentation of the information that's hard, that I'm not used to, because I've always felt, well up until this year, I would probably never do presentations in my life! I never liked getting up in front of people, so getting up in front of a class of who knows how many kids because of class sizes, let's say, 35 maybe, that I don't know, will be hard. I have to teach them something that they may or may not know about. At least in art there's much broadness and there's always new things happening and old things that are being found, new interpretations, but I still feel like I don't know a lot, you can't do the whole thing and say, 'I know everything!'

I don't even know what grade I'm going to get yet. I would love to have a Grade 8 class. I used to think I would want to teach Grade 10, 11, 12 and in this moment now, Grade 8's would be really good because they are still scared! Then I could work my way up. So even that perspective has changed in the last month and a half, of where I'd rather be. This is going to sound really bad, but I'd rather feel a little older than the kids, because Grade 8's, that's manageable for me. I'm nine, ten years older than them. I have a good chunk of time, and I'd have a little more control obviously because they're new. Control doesn't have to be in the sense of you do this, you do that, but having classroom management. I never thought my favourites would be the Grade 8's. I always thought that Grade 6, 7, 8, 9's were really snotty, and didn't want to pay attention and didn't want to work, but when I observed a Grade 8 class on our field visit, they were the best. I couldn't believe it!

The more I talk about things, the better I feel. I'm one of those people that has to walk around the mountain quite a few times, but each time I feel little bit better. I find my steps each time around, and with each of those steps, I get little bit more wisdom, and every time I go around I get another piece of the puzzle, and finally after ten or fifteen times, I get it.

Walking over the bridge

There are a lot of words I would like to use, such as frustrated, stressful, but I figure in the spirit of being positive, there was just so much happening and it was just such a whirlwind, it is hard to explain it all. There were moments when really inspiring things happened, and moments of real encouragement. There were moments of tension, and fear, and my first teaching was eighty minutes of fear because my teacher left! The students had berries that they were throwing. So anyways, other than that, I guess it was very surreal in a lot of ways and the biggest thing I learned was that teaching is not a pedestal job. I've always seen teaching as a category that takes a long time to obtain. The "teacher" was a huge heading and the teachers who do teach, they are so noble, they do such great things and they inspire kids, they encourage kids, they are monuments in kids' lives really. Now that I'm there, the job has totally been taken off the pedestal. I'm experiencing it from a low-end up, so I'm in an awkward position where I have to learn just like in any job and it's not, from where I'm seeing right now, it's not as noble as I thought it would be. I don't mean that in a negative way, but I have obtained it, it's not an unattainable position, and that really surprised me. That took me aback. Now to be able to say that I am the teacher, it is something that I guess, I never saw myself taking the step.

Teaching can happen in such different ways than I expected. I needed to see where the kids were going and what they were doing so when I was teaching them in the next week, I would know as much as I could. With my teacher I didn't feel a lot of context happening, and I didn't see the same creativity that I expected, I guess going to that pedestal ideal now, something that has taken its place is the perfect lesson. Because I have all these things I want to do and I want to teach, I would like to get the kids to be so involved, and I'm kind of reaching for that now and I saw bits and pieces of those things happening but not to the extent that I want them to happen. I want that idolized position now because I will always be trying to attain it, but as our professors have said, they never teach a perfect lesson or perfect day or perfect week or perfect month, things always happen that you don't expect.

I thought I would teach and the kids would be pumping out this great stuff. I come in with a hook, role assignment, and we are going to do teacher action plans, we're going to talk about what we are going to do, we are going to include context and image development, and elements and principles. The kids are going to be excited and discuss things, then we are going to work, and cleanup and that's how it is all going to work! There aren't going to be any tables where kids aren't working and they're all going to be excited because they are going to be able to do their own projects. In reality, the kids that are self-motivated were that and the kids that didn't care just sat there.

It was a shock, right there. One kid brought his basketball to class and he just bounced it the whole class. And then there's those certain kids who may have been ESL, there were quite a few ESL kids in the class, and I didn't know if they understood or not, or if they just didn't want to do the work. There were so many different things. They would sit there and during one lesson I taught, I had directions up on an overhead, I talked about what we were going to do, and then I went over to their table and said, "OK, we've already talked about it twice, how are you guys doing?" And they hadn't taken their sketchbooks out yet! So how can you then motivate those sorts of kids? I found that was something I really focused on. I call them the kids at risk. Then I got the Grade 8's to work in groups of four or five and that was really hard for them because some of the groups worked well, other groups didn't know what to do and they would sit there and shrug. I think good teachers make it look easy.

I did some marking for my teacher, but I didn't ever see the criteria. I'm assuming there must've been some criteria. Some kids just had their name and decorated the letters. Some kids went all out and did a whole full-blown picture and included their names, so when I was asked to mark based on which one I liked best, it was very, very hard because there obviously were some kids that had put a lot of effort into the execution of their work. The colors were great, they were really deep, things were outlined that needed to be outlined, and if you held it up from far away you'd be able to see the right things and the composition was great. And then there were the kids that probably did the criteria, put down their name, coloured it in and they're done. How can you give the person who did all the extra effort an A or A+, and the other person who did what they were supposed to, how can you not give them an A+ too? I need to have criteria, out of 10, out of 10, out of 10. And I'm a woman so there are things that look more aesthetically pleasing to me than to a man. There was one folder in particular that had a race car, the RPMs, and the boy's name in letters that implied movement. It was a great piece for him but it didn't inspire me in any way. So how can you really level that in terms of marking? I would mark much differently. I think it would be important at the beginning of the year to give the kid the syllabus, and say this is what we're going to be doing. I would have an overall marking scheme for every single thing they do. We'd go over it so they always know what is expected.

I often stayed until 6 o'clock like some of the teachers at the school. It would be much more advantageous for me to be there until maybe 4:30, help cleanup and then say, "I'm going to go home to work on my lesson plans." I didn't really want to stay late all the time, but I felt I had to. My teacher helps with a number of clubs, but I've never been big on dancing, so staying for the salsa club, I'm doing it because she does it. She asked, "Can you make a poster for me for the salsa club?" So I made a poster, and it became assumed that I was going to stay. I left early because my feet hurt so bad from all day, and I felt so bad after, I felt so awful. The whole way back on the bus I thought, '*Oh I should have just stayed, why, what propelled me to go home?*' In the moment it was the selfishness of my feet, my feet hurt. It made me grumpy so I just went home without really thinking about what I was doing. And I really wanted to have my own space. I didn't want to show anybody my frown. I felt I would've snapped at anybody if they had talked to me. I wanted to go see my husband. I didn't want to make any tensions or any uncomfortableness at the school.

I was surprised at how tired I was every day. I know that sounds a little bit negative, but teaching is a very wearing job. You need to have enough of yourself to go home and still be yourself. It was pretty easy for me to go home, take off my shoes and get in my pyjamas. I think taking your clothes off and putting on your home self is very important. Every day I would have an hour to watch TV or I would play on the computer a little bit, or I would do something that was not work related at all, and that really helped me get into it. I don't know how people go about having a private life after being in school and being so busy all day. My sister visited us during the first week. She helped me pick out my clothes for the next day. She ironed for me once or twice. Teaching the second week and not having her there was hard. I think we ordered pizza almost every night because I didn't have time, and I was too tired making my lessons every night and doing a PowerPoint. It took three or four hours, so you take an hour of rest time, make dinner, and I wanted to be in bed by 11 p.m., but I wouldn't get to bed until 12 a.m. or 12:30 a.m. every night.

Before we went on practicum, it was drilled into our heads, Code 5, Code 5, Code 5 – don't speak ill about anybody. Be as positive as you can out there, if not too positive. Make every effort to smile at anybody you see, you say hi to everyone, you butter them up, you make yourself look the best you can. Sometimes on the practicum, things said to me were very surprising. I couldn't believe it. Teachers break Code 5 and you automatically become part of a private space. I didn't like that. I don't want to make any assumptions about anybody, and as student-teachers, we need to be extra careful about all the codes. So how we answer that is by keeping it to ourselves. If we make that public, it will create a certain atmosphere around us, around the teacher who told us in the first place, and then it could take any direction. I didn't like that at all. I'm a person who can keep secrets but I don't like keeping secrets especially between me and my husband. I don't think there should be any behind-the-scenes talk in an institution where you are working with everybody so closely together all the time. There is a real, oh, what is the word, hierarchy of people, and there's a lot of animosity from the people who don't have the positions they want in schools.

One of the teachers talked to me because he wasn't sure if he was going to take me on or not. I said, "I'll do anything just let me stay!" He recognized right away that I wasn't really putting my opinions out there. I was saying, "I'll do whatever you like, where can I fit in?" That's how I perceived myself to be most useful, because then they can say just go here or go there and what he wanted to hear was, I can do this, let me do this part at this time in this class. He wanted straight up answers rather than agreement.

He said to me, "You have to be really careful because you can give of yourself until there is nothing left to give because there are always people who will want your help."

When I'm in a public role I always try to watch what I say, I try to be very politically correct, which is hard. I'm nervous to put out my opinions because I'm a harmonious person so when I'm in public, I'm the most people pleasing I possibly can be, and that really showed during the practicum. When I was out during the practicum, my teacher would ask whatever, I had no boundaries really and that is something I have to work on. Life as a teacher really depends on the reference letter your sponsor teacher writes for you, and as bad as that may sound, you have to make sure everything you do is in line with what they think and I don't want to ruffle any feathers. I always ask my sponsor teacher, "What do you think about this?"

I think I gave the impression to the kids that I'm a very serious person. I have to smile more, even though I'm trying to distance myself, I still need to be very approachable and I don't think I showed that very well. I even wrote that on my lesson plan – smile – so that I would remember. Going back to the whole idea of the bridge, I recognize in myself that I'm a real perfectionist and that came out in my teaching skills because I wanted my first lesson to be perfect and I wanted every lesson after that to be perfect too. So when my faculty advisor came to watch me, I felt very pressured to be perfect and I don't even know what perfect is. Even in other instances in my life, earlier on the bridge, or walking over the bridge, I've always been scared because it's not perfect and that's usually why I don't go forward. So in teaching a lot of things go wrong and learning from them is needed to get better, but it was a painful period of learning. I would've rather walked around the pond, taken the long way, but really I know that theory doesn't help after a certain point. You have to practice using it. The short practicum didn't change me, it fortified the idea of identity, that you need to have a public time and then there's time when you have to go home. You have to let go for the day and then go fresh in the morning. I was really nervous those two weeks, really tense. My faculty advisor said I need to relax more and have fun.

I had a kind of out of body experience in that first lesson I taught. My mind wasn't thinking about the lesson, it was completely thinking about when the lesson was done. It was the time factor, there were forty minutes left and these kids weren't listening to me. It was really hard. My brain was racing and the body was kind of there, my mind was totally in the moment. I just wanted time to be up so bad. I wanted the teacher to come back and take control so I could go sit down and watch some more. So that first experience with the Grade 8's, it was very scary. I did not want to be there in that moment! But by the second day, it was almost the opposite. We made masks. They couldn't finish the lesson because they were rowdy, but they had so much fun and I almost felt like a big sister. You have to be careful about that line, but I felt really comfortable with them and I was able to walk around and say, "How are you doing?" It was fun. I was surprised the first day took so long, and the second day was so fast. Having the time go by fast is much better.

I learned I'm very interested in assessment. I did my own marking for the two-day project that I did. I had a criteria that was ten marks for creativity, ten marks for group work, ten for use of material because it was earth art, and ten for a written paragraph that each student had to write. We did a self-assessment and most of them graded themselves quite honestly, which was very exciting. I really enjoyed that. Most of the paragraphs were very good. I had them answer whether it was 2-dimensional or 3-dimensional, what they did, why it was earth art, what materials they used and I got them to explain what the work was because that's how they were going to document their work. And I took pictures. It was really great.

I also had an experience that fortified the idea that I can just be who I am as a teacher. I saw some students in the library doing a project on war and peace, and one student was drawing a picture of an apple and a sword, and I saw the apple and I thought, '*Oh, I wonder if that's what I think it is*,' and I went and asked her. Now looking back right at this moment, that could've been putting the student on the spot because it was about her faith. Had a teacher asked me, I would have shied away.

She said, "I was thinking about the original sin and how that's the idea of war and peace."

For me, to hear that from a student, because she obviously holds the same beliefs as I do, that really encouraged me that kids will, what's the word, they will allow themselves to express that in art. I did that when I was in high school and I worked through some very difficult issues. For her to be working through that in a similar way really inspired me; you are free to express yourself if you want to in schools. I would really encourage that if students want to try. It was really cool for me.

When we came back from our short practicum, we talked about all the positive stuff, and I was really appreciative of that, for me it was really really helpful to pull out all those positive things. It made me feel better about what I had done. It was good to be back at university. Hearing from other people was really what I needed so that was just great in reinforcing that yes, I still want to be a teacher. From what I heard, I had a better experience than a lot of people. There were some things that people probably needed to talk about and they didn't think they were allowed, so everyone was getting a little antsy. It is also the end of the term and everybody's stressed. For others it would have been helpful to hear some encouraging words like "It's okay, this is the hardest part, we'll work through it together, and we're all here to support you and keep going, keep trying."

Coming back to the cohort and being able to wear jeans and sweats, it feels nice, but I'm starting to notice there is a professional me and then there's the comfortable me. I think I took a lot more time thinking about what I was going to wear than anybody else, and it wasn't because I'm a vain person, but because fashion is not me. I like comfortableness, but I really felt I had to look professional and I had to just make myself stand out. Every night I had at least a twenty minute stare in my closet trying to figure out what was going to match. How could I wear my blazer? I couldn't wear jeans and I couldn't wear khakis, so what was I going to do. I want to have fun jewellery, which I don't have, so every morning I would wear some earrings, or make sure my hair looks nice, and that in itself stressed me out because I wanted to look different. I had this amazing revelation just yesterday because we went observing to an independent school and again, I wore black slacks, a pink sweater, and a gray blazer. So I dressed for the part, perfectly. I went to the bathroom at one point and I caught myself in a full-length mirror in the school and I kind of stood there for a second and I thought, '*I really do look exactly how I want*.' It made me realize that I was really successful in this goal and I got comments throughout the two weeks on practicum like "You know, you look really nice today." Let's say it gave me a little sense of peace.

I am the paintbrush

As a spiritual person I want to imitate Christ in my life and the way I'm living my life, so I want my spirit to embody Jesus, which means I'm humble, very humble, very wanting to learn along with students, being a learner with them. The biggest thing I want is to love the kids. I want to make sure that I'm someone they feel comfortable with. Since the short practicum, how I approach my work as a student is different. As a student, it is easy to procrastinate, which is a bad thing. This is still part of my mindset. With a job like teaching, you might be at the end of the year, your kids are finished, but you've got so much still to do.

I wonder how much time I'm going to actually have during the winter break to do art. I haven't been doing a lot of art, just a lot of writing in my visual journal. My mother-in-law and father-in law bought me a movable easel for my birthday so I'm very excited about that. I have a sense that I'm going to be helping kids in their learning now and they can be the canvas, and I'm the paintbrush. I want to do art, but there's so much other stuff happening. There's work that needs to be done so I'm ready for the long practicum. It is hard to make sure that I'm the wife and have all the qualities, how do I say this, the ten most important things that a wife and husband need. I always want to make sure that I'm loving him, taking care of him and he would do the same with me. I'm very preoccupied because I'm a new wife too. I want to make sure I'm doing things for us, and making time for each other. I really feel it is important because I'm busy and he's busy. During my two-week practicum it was really difficult. He had a really difficult week because he's taking courses, his electives, and he experienced the all-night paper, along with a presentation and his thesis presentation the same weekend, and another paper, so that was a hard week. At a certain point you don't really know how to help anymore and I'm sure he probably felt the same way with me and my practicum. We're learning those ins and outs.

I want to embody the pedagogical practices of a teacher so I'm working towards that and it is taking time. I think I take on too much sometimes. Our professors pump us up so much, saying, "You can do this." And I wonder, *'How am I going to do it?'* Schools aren't always going to have the supplies you want to use, and if you want to have intense discussions with your students, you need to know them first before you can have those discussions. Say for instance, we were talking about Disney movies. Are they good for your kids? I was a Disney kid so that was really hard for me! I don't step on people's toes, so even though I might think otherwise I really don't say. I have my own opinions in class but I don't share them because there was a very 'for' side and a very 'against' side and either way, if I said something, I was going to have to pick a side. So I kept quiet. I mean I have my own points and people were already commenting on that so I just stayed neutral. It could be great to talk about this in your classroom, why something is good to watch, or why it is bad, but you can't just go in there and put on a movie and say, "What do you think?" Their minds aren't as developed as mine so they're going to have a different debate than in my university classroom, which was very heated. Sometimes kids don't want to talk about public things, they want to keep to themselves, so how do you have a discussion then? A teacher has to be really careful about the debates you are going to have, or the art projects you are going to do.

I'm also thinking about what my classroom would look like in the future. I'm doing a unit on spaces right now. We talked about this briefly in class and someone said they would like to have a couch in their classroom. So I was thinking about that all day and I think it is such a great idea to have a couch in the art room. Could I have a Nintendo there to make it a more comfortable space? Does that cross the line? I know I'd be right there playing!

The long practicum went really well

For the first week of my long practicum, I was quite timid.

Then one of my sponsor teachers said, "Even if you don't feel confident, you need to give off the impression of being so, because the kids pick up on it and don't behave."

Boy is that true! The next lesson I was much stricter, and ended up having a wonderful discussion with my kids about colours and emotions. We moved into how the classroom feels with certain colours, what bedroom colours usually are, and we did colour theory, which is like the periodic table, where perspective and tone and value are equations that students need. I asked everyone to participate, everyone paid attention, and there were some who had a great time! It was really neat to see immediate results. Students were thinking about concepts and then participating.

I learned a few things about myself as a teacher. I can get very stressed out if I create unrealistic expectations but still expect to get them done. I'm not ready to improvise as of yet. And when kids don't listen and wait time doesn't work, what do I do? I really want my class to be organized, none of this papers everywhere or students not being able to find stuff. There were times I had to be quite strict with some of my students. All the teachers and advisors told me that they have to know who the boss is.

One sponsor teacher said, "If a male teacher is strict or mean, the students respect him. If a woman is strict or mean, she is automatically a bitch."

You need to be able to find a balance, so your students know when you mean business and when you are being a friend or confidante. During my practicum, I did see this strategy play out successfully. I also found that if I have a constructive criticism for a student's work, if it is given on a more private level, with positive points to sandwich it, they are usually very receptive to change. I had a student or two who didn't want to be at school. Therefore they didn't have anything to say to me, and constructive words, or encouragement seemed to fall on deaf ears. I believe a couple of times I received a smile, or a short 'thanks,' which was by far most rewarding. Because I'm young, I find it particularly easy to relate to students. For example, one group of students was talking about Nintendo and DDR, Dance Dance Revolution, and how it was so much fun. Well, my husband and I still play Nintendo and recently we bought "DDR." I felt however, that I should not engage in that conversation with students. I don't know yet what constitutes boundaries or not, that would have been more friendship and less teacher. The other major difference was the amount of responsibility I had all of a sudden.

I did a 'concept of the day' where I gave a small demo and answered questions, something I've just learned how to do. For the first half of the week I forgot to ask if there were any questions, and the kids just got right to work! My students had a passion for art, and their imaginations got to work very promptly. I did student self-evaluations every class so they told me what they liked and didn't like about the lesson, and rating the class on a 1 to 5 scale, with 1 being worst and 5 being best. I got a lot of comments saying they just wanted to make art; however, I also got a lot of comments saying they really enjoyed the lessons. I find that those self-evaluations are one of the best ways to see if the students have engaged in learning, because their comments, short or lengthy, really gave me a sense of what they thought the lesson was about, and whether they liked it or not.

I learned that attendance isn't important to do right away. I like doing attendance once they've started work. Sometimes it's good to do as a classroom management skill. In my own classroom, I think it would be nice to have sketchbook time every class for fifteen minutes. My teachers in high school did that for my Grade 11/12 years, and it always worked to get my creative juices going. They would give us a topic for the week, and we had to work on it all week long. My sponsor teachers don't do this for their own reasons. Sometimes, I'm finding that it's okay to just make an announcement about what the day is for, catch up, work period, etcetera, and then after half the class, do a short demo, so if the students are finished, or need some new thoughts, that shakes things up so to speak.

I try very hard to shape my questions so that I encourage upper level thinking. I'm not sure how successful I am at that yet, but it is usually in the back of my mind. I know that in the objectives for each day, in terms of creating/communicating or perceiving/responding, they are working towards upper level thinking activities such as creating their own ideas. I also encourage upper level thinking through my self-evaluations. I usually encourage students as I walk around, but if I see a problem, I ask them if I can give them a suggestion. Really, if they don't want to accept what I have to say, I'm wasting my time as well as theirs. Many of the students will ask me what I think, which is an open door for me to then ask them, "Well, what do you think? Are you happy with your current outcome? Where do you think some trouble areas might be?" Now that I know most of the kids by name, I can have a bit of a conversation with them, and that makes a world of difference. My comments now have some validity to them. They know I know what I'm talking about and they produce amazing work!

I think getting into a routine is also a big part of this job. You have to know where you're at, what you're marking, what you're teaching next, and you need to be organized. I've tried really hard to be organized, but there are always things you can do better. With my faculty advisor, we often talk about classroom management, since that is one area I'm having trouble with. In one class, I barely had control of the students the whole time, but it was a GREAT learning experience for me. It gave me the opportunity to talk over classroom management with all three of my sponsor teachers, and think about it myself. The next lesson I implemented their suggestions and the results were amazing. It felt good to be in control, not like a dictator, but authoritatively, and to have the students listen when I talked, and vice versa. The tone and the atmosphere of the class changed for the better. I think a good teacher evaluates fairly, relates well with kids, turns kids on to learning, is flexible, provides ways for success and management, knows there is more than one learning style, doesn't show stage fright, and has compassion and cares.

I'm just starting a new unit plan with my Grade 8's, and I did a small lecture on art history using classical, renaissance, ready-made and cubist references, showing the students the idea of shape, how it works in a composition, how shapes are used to build bodies and how the master painters have done this. *The Last Supper* is so wonderful for this! Anyways, the students were all very engrossed in the lesson, and I think they all really enjoyed it. I think it's important to fix the concept or technique within them, so that they can 'break the rules' so to speak. After they have mastered the technique they are learning, the final project is their time to shine. Although there are guidelines such as use two of the four techniques we've been learning about, or neatness, or whatever, they can still create their own project, and I get the opportunity to watch them work. I find it very helpful to have students write an artist statement after large projects. My Grade 8's just wrote an artist statement on shoe transformations, but they had to write a story about how their shoe was transformed, where it was born, what did it do, almost as if the shoe was magic. They loved it! I think that developing the students' skills in art is one of the most important things an art teacher teaches. I teach in small lessons, usually no longer than ten minutes, and then I give them activities that I hope they find fun, and that helps them practice.

My private life affected my practicum in positive ways. My husband keeps me upbeat more than I realize. My husband is extremely positive and supportive about my experiences and often offered helpful suggestions or read over my ideas. When I stayed late, or had homework prep for the next day, he understood and helped where he could. He asked me to be finished by 9 p.m. every night so we could have time together. Although hard to do at first, this helped me learn how to time manage quite effectively. I was motivated to finish before that time. It helped me stay on task, to get done what was necessary for the next day, not necessarily the next week. Weekends were a good time for me to prep a bit extra for the coming week. If I was diligent, I could plan up to Wednesday, which then helped free up time during the week. I wouldn't say that there weren't stressful nights. My sleep patterns changed, thus my husband's sleeping patterns changed. We were up at 7 a.m. He had to deal with a tired and sometimes grumpy wife if I didn't get to bed on time.

I would have to argue that my practicum was probably one of the best experiences I've had. I had a fantastic time. The long practicum went really well. The weeks went by so fast and it was so much fun. I had great sponsor teachers, a wonderful, helpful faculty advisor and great kids, not to mention a supportive husband, family and God! My practicum was a very caring experience. My sponsor teachers were there to help me and encouragement was given far more often than criticism, and we were often in collaboration. I wasn't kept sitting on a problem. Of course, I tried very hard to make this atmosphere work as well. I tried to be as flexible as possible. I asked opinions and advice of my teachers rather than going on my own opinions, and part of my final evaluation took this into account. I participated a great deal in the life of the school, in clubs, attending meetings and more. I got along well with the school staff and I thoroughly enjoyed the kids and my classes. I liked feeling that I was the facilitator, that students were learning things I was teaching, and seeing process and product. Each day was different and exciting. One of my teachers wanted to team-teach with me through the entirety of my time there, which helped with the rough patches since she did most of the disciplining. The other two left me to my own devices, which allowed me to expand on my understanding of teaching. It was a lot of work being the teacher! Just recently, my sponsor teacher who is retiring allowed me to go through all her lesson plans and take what I wanted, and she sold some of her art books to me at a fantastic price. I was really excited. As well, she and I have kept in touch by email and she has let me know that if I ever need ideas or help or advice, or just someone to talk to, she'd love to keep in touch. I'm very lucky. Now my husband is looking into education as a profession.

There's a new bridge to cross

I'm feeling very happy to be done for lots of reasons. It has been such a long year and not having a summer has been really hard especially seeing everyone else do whatever they like. Now it feels as though there's a new bridge to cross. I'm finished the program and I have a long-term job, something I've never had before, something I've always wanted. But between the end of school and starting a job, there is no time. I have my week of holidays and then I have two weeks to get ready for a job. Two weeks is not a lot of time. I'm feeling a bit burned out. I'm looking forward to doing nothing for a day or two.

I have new fears arising, as fast as the excitement! I do know however that I have much more confidence and it won't be so hard as beginning the first practicum. I now have resources and contacts and I have learned how to be flexible with what comes my way. I feel as though I have grown significantly in this moment of being a student, versus now being a teacher. It is a very new feeling. Thinking back to the actual job interview, I did feel comfortable in the space, and I felt that I was a qualified individual for the job at hand.

As a teacher of art I hope to inspire creativity and a love of learning during my lessons. I will encourage student participation as much as possible and set reachable objectives that hopefully will be interesting to my students. I feel very passionate about what I teach. With a new class, sometimes it is important to be a bit strict, but encouraging students to ask questions is good. I love to walk around and compliment students on their work. I find it gives me a bit of a personal connection with them. They like to talk about what they are doing, and the majority of the time, conversations lead to life outside of the classroom. Once I have my own classroom, I would hope to do more group assignments to encourage student relationships. I would move kids periodically to also help relationships develop and I believe more importantly, I would like to develop a sense of respect for everyone and every artwork produced. One of my sponsor teachers did 'walk abouts' which I believe was good for students, to see each other's work as well as learn different styles. Organizing the classroom as a gallery space would also help create a community of practice.

I talked to the director of the school and the art teacher that I will be working with, and they are both lovely people. I'm really excited. It is going to be a great working atmosphere. I feel there are a lot of expectations. I think the expectations are coming in little increments, and I'm only beginning to understand what sort of a school it is. It's not just a practicum anymore. I really have to be good at what I'm doing now. When I talked to the director, we talked about parents a little bit. I had read in their magazine about students who were in major productions internationally, and their parents are CEOs.

The director said, "Well you have to remember that when the parents come to the school, they are the mom or the dad."

But it is still pretty intimidating. One of the reasons I want to go into the independent school system is because I want the parent involvement. I find that so important and lacking in public schools. So I'm excited about this!

The other teacher is also really friendly and they are going to buddy-me-up so that I have a mentor. The first day of school is a big Pro-D day for us to get to know each other and figure out how the school works, and the more I thought about it, the better off I am having a smaller position because I get to learn it. I'm looking forward to concentrating on four classes a week, doing them well, and building on what I know. I'm pretty excited but at the same time I don't want this to go to my head either. It's great to have a position in that school but I don't want it to become, '*I* work here,' you know? I think that could be so detrimental. I went into an independent school for certain reasons, but it wasn't to become better than people, and stereotypes get pushed onto people all the time, so I don't want people to look at me that way. I told two people in the cohort about the job, just out of pure excitement, but I found out later, one of them had failed and the other person hasn't been hired at all. So then I felt bad afterwards but they were excited for me that I had a job. I realize I'm pretty lucky. After coming back to the cohort for the final term, I found that I had been particularly fortunate in my experience on the practicum too. Many of my classmates had horrible experiences far beyond what I think is fair or professional. I had it really good and I consequently felt bad talking about my experiences.

This reminds me of my friend who has been a teacher for about five years now.

I have talked to her and it was so funny, she said, "Doesn't it feel great when you know you're supposed to be a teacher? It's exactly where you want to be and every day is a great day."

I mean, obviously there are mistakes, but you learn, and it's exactly where you're supposed to be. It is just fantastic! I remember when she went through her education program and some of the things she said then have really resonated with me since, about the idea that not everyone is going to make it, and hearing about people in her program that were just not cut out for it. It is funny now to start thinking about that and to see the parallels.

On my practicum I was removed from the rest because I didn't have an art specialist, I had a generalist faculty advisor. When everyone got back, no one wanted to talk about anything. It was just, 'How was your practicum? Good. And how was yours? Good.' It is only in this last term that people have started coming out and saying, actually it wasn't that good, or they didn't do so well. Somehow we talk. I know that support and sympathy is needed, and I think I do sometimes exhibit those traits and people see that.

Our final day in the program was anticlimactic. We were done and that was it. Because we were a cohort for so long, it felt weird that the actual last day was last term. This term we weren't all in the same class, so it wasn't a good-bye. There was no final 'See you around!' Certain people had parties and some people were left out of that too, and me being one of the people. I never really made really good friends with anybody. I was on good terms with everybody. So I was a floater. We are now all doing our own thing and people are going to get jobs and people are going to move. Some people are going to have kids. So I don't feel a particular landmark I guess, it is not 'The End.' There are these group emails, 'Oh it's all over, it is so sad.' And I think, *'Oh great, another sappy email to read!'* I'm more focused on jobs. The end for me was more at the end of the practicum. I became much better friends with the group that was at my school and I think because it was such a different way of learning than in the university classroom, we were all learning to be teachers together. There were a couple of people there that I will keep in contact with and see how they're doing and I know they've got jobs. What you have done this year, and how hard you have worked is now showing and I guess it depends on how much you wanted it.

How does my dad say it, "If you fail to plan then you plan to fail."

In the last term of this program, I discovered even further that I hate conceptual art. It is so academic and it is so exclusive. No one can understand it. I really don't like it. And if I want to make an art piece during one of my courses, it had to be conceptual, and that was a second frustration for me. I can't make art and I'm in the art program! Conceptual ideas do not come easily to me. I like a painting because it looks nice! When I think about art, my motto should come from that movie, *You've Got Mail*. It has to start by being personal. I make art for myself but if I want to make it for a viewer or an audience, I will make it for a viewer or an audience. It also creates a conflict for me because it's one thing to teach identity and whatever you like in high school but how does that prepare students for university art? I find that really frustrating. I will be teaching Grades 6 and 7, so I don't have to be worried about that until next year, but if I'm going to teach those grades later on, in order to keep students in the loop and help them move forward, I'll have to teach conceptual art, but that is not why people go into art usually. It's not to be part of this elite group. It's because they enjoy expressing themselves in a different way. I don't think there's anything wrong with art being narrative.

I'm asking myself some life questions now. I'm really happy the program is done but I'm not coming back to university unless I choose to do so later on. If I were to do a Master's, I would do it in art evaluation. I'm starting what I want to do for the rest of my life. I hope it is going to be everything that I wanted it to be. I know one of my friends and I have often talked about how you grow up a lot when you start your job. So I wonder how much I'm going to change now. I love art and I believe this comes through in my teaching and I'll benefit from teaching this subject as will my students. I will learn new things every day. I teach to the kid's freedom of expression. The teacher education program has stretched and moulded me in ways I could not have imagined. I have walked, crawled, and run over many bridges in the process of learning what it means to be a teacher. As a teacher, I am building my own bridge of student and personal success. Every student cannot be reached, but it is my responsibility as a teacher to try. My experiences on practicum have already started this bridge. I am often frightened by bridges, and this one I am about to build is no different. I believe though that I will build self-confidence with each experience. One of the greatest things about becoming a teacher is the fact that I will be a lifelong learner and that is exciting to me. My bridge will never finish, so mistakes and experiences will only make my journey more interesting. I accept this opportunity with vigour and excitement. Let the building begin!

CHAPTER 2

UNEXPECTEDNESS:
ANN'S STORY

It runs in my blood

I love art and it is the only thing I can see myself doing for the rest of my life. I've always had a big interest in education programs and education in general, and I would like to make some big changes, where it lacks and where it is strong. It runs in my blood. I have lots of family working in the education system. My whole family is very artistic as well. I have two aunts who are teachers, another is an administrator, some cousins in teacher training and my mom was a teacher's assistant and First Nations counsellor-type person, but I came here for my own reasons. I think I would like to see more diverse teachers because I remember going through school and it was all European descent and everybody taught and thought the same way and I got really bored with it. The only people of cultural or ethnic diversity were working as First Nations coordinators, counsellors or in alternative education.

I thought I was going to have to jump through the hoops here. I thought I'd have to conform to the traditional teaching methods, but those are sort of starting to go out the window. I was hoping to get rid of them in my own fashion, as I teach. I thought I would have to just get through this school and pretend to do what they want me to do, and then do my own thing, but it seems it is starting in the right direction. The constructivist methods of teaching are totally in line with what I am thinking. I thought I was going to have to hide that part of me, so it's great. It always seemed like with the teachers, even the ones I had at university, this is the way it's done, and you do it this way, very sequential. I liked my art classes in high school, and that inspired me to be a teacher because it was more random and fun. I could be myself and explore my own interests. It was a break from everything else, like those academic courses that focus on memorization. Even some of those teachers inspired me. I had a science teacher who would randomly do crazy things and it kept us interested, rather than just learning through blah, blah, blah, and write, write, write, which is really boring. I want to change that and make the school more interesting for people. I like teachers that are like that.

I decided to become an art teacher for so many reasons, but the main reasons are that I see the potential of the art classroom in including and educating students in all areas of life from history to science, architecture, design, human studies, and the list goes on. I see the art class as a great place for students to find themselves and their place in this world. I also have a passion for creating art and learning from art. On a more personal note, I am a member of the Lheidli T'enneh band. I grew up on some land on the side of the Nechako River just out of the city limits. Here I developed a close relationship with the natural world, which greatly informs my art practice and worldview.

When I went to public school, I was always striving to be the top of the class. I was always in the top 5% or 10%, and if my marks went down it bothered me. I wasn't quite the teacher's pet. I was the one that would sit quietly, do my homework and try to get it done before class was finished because I didn't like homework. I had other things to do! I was a pretty quiet student. I took Toastmasters a couple of times. I was always considered the observer-type learner. There was a year, around Grade 9, that I went off the deep end. I got really bored with school. It was the same thing every year. We were learning the same things. I thought, *'Why even bother? I'm not learning anything, it's so repetitive and if I get my homework done before the class is even over, am I really learning anything?'* So I had a hard time with that, with the classes, and being motivated to go there. And then, I don't know, I started doing drugs for about a year and stopped. I don't know what it was, I started skipping classes. I thought, *'I'm not learning anything anyways, I'm not missing anything.'* I was still going to pass the tests and I was able to keep up with the class when I got back. I managed to keep my grades up to a decent 'B' for a long time. I went through a period where I started doing drugs really heavily and didn't go at all, and my grades went down. I still did homework and still got the tests done, but that was minimal, and my grades went down just because the teachers decided

I wasn't taking it seriously. So when my grades went down deep, it knocked me back and it worked. My grades went from an 'A' to a 'C,' and bam, I was back at school again.

There was always high stress in my family as well. Maybe I put more pressure on myself than anybody else. I grew up in an all-white family. My sisters and I are the only Natives or persons of non-European decent. We didn't know any of our Native half, only the French-Italian half, and they are all really high academics and we always felt like they look down on us. My mom's half, the Native half, they all grew up in really small communities and most of them got into the drugs and alcohol and just can't seem to come out of it. So I'm actually kind of grateful that I wasn't in contact with them all the time. I have a feeling it would've been a bad influence. But also now, I'm starting to feel my place in the world more. There was a moment when I realized I'm different and that's why the family treated me so, and then once I realized how different I was, it made me really insecure for a long time. So I just try to stick to myself and try to do my best to prove everyone wrong about what they thought about me, and little things that happened, that probably had nothing to do with the fact that I was Native, that's because of this or that.

When I thought about getting into the teaching program, one of my main reasons was that the only First Nations people employed in the education system were always in counselling or First Nations studies, never in an administrative position, and that bothered me. I thought, you know, we can do more than that and we are needed in more places than that. We need First Nations people teaching history because history is not told properly and we need them to teach everything else, so that we can prove that we can do it, and to influence First Nations students who want to do those things. We can teach things in different ways that make things connect. It's one of my main goals. I want to try and inspire people to expand their horizons.

When I was in school, there were a lot of First Nations people who would say, "I can work in the mill after, nobody's going to hire me anyways so why should I bother."

It is pretty bad. It is true in a lot of cases that people are not hired because of their race or appearance.

I remember I went home for Christmas and I went into a store to buy some art supplies. I found what I was looking for and then someone asked me to empty my pockets. I was just shocked.

I replied, "Seriously? OK." I was a little embarrassed and shocked, and I thought, '*What the hell!*' So I emptied my pockets and I was really embarrassed.

She said, "Okay, sorry, I just had to ask because I thought I saw you stealing."

So I left the store really mad. I ended up having to go back because it was the only store that had what I needed in town. I was biting my tongue when I went back, thinking I should be talking to the supervisor, but I thought, you know, it really wouldn't go that far. I know, honestly, that's as far as it is going to go. It's just common around here. That is when I realized that how I dress and how I act makes a big difference in how people treat me, which is really sad. I started playing with my image for a while. Sometimes I dress down just to test people. I want to wear whatever I want, but then I realize how much a public image you are in teaching. Now I've started feeling I'm like a teacher, I'm more aware of how people perceive me, even my own friends, instructors, family. It doesn't matter what situation you're in, dress makes a difference. I have always had the impression that if I was to ever lose a sense, I would rather lose sight. I wish everybody else would too. We rely on eyesight too much and make assumptions from it. I would still be an artist and still trying to be an art teacher even if I was blind!

When I went to art school, I tried a little of everything because I wanted to be a teacher, so I wanted to know as much as I could, planning to teach those methods. Not many people did that actually. In art school, we were expected to develop our own style and in the end, I did have my own style. I thought all my work was really random, but after looking back on four years of work, a lot of it is connected in concepts or themes or styles. I don't like my style, but it is my style, so I go with it. At first, I did a lot of landscape painting because I missed home. But such paintings weren't highly regarded because landscape painting is dead in a conceptual art school. It is all concepts and nothing else. I could have been developing my skills with landscape art but we had this other stuff, so I learned how to bullshit my way through it to make things I wanted into conceptual pieces, which is all different points of view and seeing things differently. I just decided to start exploring other things and fine, if you are going to be conceptual, I'm not going to pass, so what do I need to do to get the grades. It was all jumping through those hoops, but that's what you expect with an education system built that way.

I want to be the kind of teacher that totally relates to the kids. I'm not going to be that old teacher telling you what to do and where to go while you're sitting there beating your head against the wall waiting for the class to end. I'm hoping to be that fun teacher. And I'm sure it's going to take a while to be what I want to be. It's just not my natural self, humorous and flamboyant, so I got to try to work on those traits. I'm just seeing things in teachers that I love, and I want to try to be more like the teachers that I like. I do want to touch on the conceptual aspects of art for sure but I don't want that to be the only theme in high school. It's just too much for high school students to have to learn. They should try to understand it, but it should not be pressured onto them to create it all the time. I like focusing on art more as a personal thing, and if you do art for therapy, for yourself, or just for the enjoyment, for the aesthetic, or if you do it to sell it, you can focus on what you want to focus on. Art doesn't have to be one certain thing.

I was excited to get into this program, very excited, because I love to learn things. I feel I can learn much more than in my previous degree in art. I'm learning about education and people, I'm taking courses on adolescents, special needs and stuff like that, so I'm hoping to learn a lot. I was excited, but I was scared. It's a big school, compared to my old one, and new people. I was afraid of taking seven courses. How was I ever going to do this when I've done five courses tops, and they were pretty slack?

Most of my family and friends, they were excited. They knew I had planned this out for a few years now. This is what I was going to do. Everybody said, "You are going to be a great teacher!" And I thought wow, that's so encouraging. People think highly of me and my abilities to teach and that kept me going. I didn't really express too much to too many people. A lot of my family still don't really know what I'm doing. My sister got married this summer and that was a good time. When socializing, I told quite a few people then but I didn't really broadcast it. I would rather them hear about my accomplishments than create expectations.

I was already nervous before I arrived at university. I was overwhelmed looking at the amount of work. I didn't know what to expect. I was very apprehensive, especially when the courses became confusing. Some courses were split between two days, and the art cohort has three core classes with three different instructors that teach four days of the week. But coming back to school wasn't too bad because I was very familiar with the city. It would have been worse if I hadn't been here before.

On the first day we met the cohort. I walked into class and I was amazed because there were five familiar faces. I wasn't with a bunch of strangers so it put me at ease a little bit because then I wouldn't have to push myself so hard to socialize with people I don't know. So I think we all felt comfortable with the familiar faces in the classroom and from there it is easy to socialize because we had things in common. We talked about what different experiences we had. The first day wasn't that bad. It wasn't till the end of the first week that I started to freak out. It was the handouts. There were piles and piles of handouts and assignments. It's hard to organize what we're supposed to have for each day and who's going to be there. I understand it now, but it was very confusing for those four days. I think I freaked out a few times and well, I broke down and cried a couple of times, thinking, '*Is this what I've paid for?*' I tried to figure out how to organize all these binders, all the different classes. I've been getting a lot of headaches lately from the stress and the confusion. It also probably has to do with health issues, like not eating well, not getting enough sleep and trying to balance academics with a personal life. I feel guilty for doing something that's not school. Then I think, '*I shouldn't be doing this!*' It is such a big headache and there is not enough time to do everything. I don't even know how I make it to all of my classes. I had a really hard time the first week getting up. There is no time for groceries, cooking, eating, or sleeping.

I just find it amazing how peoples' mindsets here are so different from mine. There's no way, even when I've tried in several different ways to explain things, for them to get it. In my courses, I see how people are marking my stuff, or not marking it, but look at what I say, and I know they don't really understand what I'm saying. It's kind of difficult dealing with that sort of situation. I'm not sure. I'm considering talking to some of the instructors, and explaining to them, maybe they'll understand me more if they know more about my history, because a lot of them just assume that I'm from here, that I grew up in the city, and even the assumption that I'm going to do my practicum here. Because I'm going far away, my experience will be totally different, and they are offering all these resources, but I'm not here to have access to them. I'll be so far away. It's interesting, some of things they say and I realize that it doesn't apply to me, so how can I make it apply? I'm enjoying learning all the skills I'm learning from the instructors. There are certain instructors that are teaching me how to teach, which is really great. My cousin, who is also in the teacher education program at this university, told me she doesn't know how to teach yet, so I'm getting all this knowledge about this and that. Actually, we're overloaded with strategies. It is so much to take in. It is hard. I'm afraid I'll forget a lot of it when the pressure is on during the next few months, just in terms of time management and health. I don't know how to deal with a classroom at this point. At first, I didn't think I could relate to young kids, although I'm starting to question that now. But secondary students are older than me in some ways, and they know more than me, so what am I going to do? And knowing how to deal with all the crazy situations that could come up and learning how to better myself in those situations will be a challenge. If I were to go into a class right now, I don't know if I could do it. I was considering finding out how demanding teaching is; I want to put everything I can into it. It might be possible that I just want to be a part-time teacher.

I just felt like I was going to a residential school or something

We went on a field visit to a high school. It was super crowded. I didn't expect to feel that crowded. The classrooms were too small, it didn't really seem too organized, and there was a bunch of clutter on

45

the walls and stuff they don't even use. I just felt it was too cluttered and especially with all the kids sitting there, nobody can move around. They didn't even have room do their work. They were sitting on top of each other with one piece of paper in front of them and they need more than that, they have all these materials, and books and backpacks and stuff. It was impossible. I'm really hoping that my classrooms aren't going to be like that, but I'm pretty sure they will be. We were observing in groups of six. It was insane. I noticed there was a lack of attention for people with disabilities. There was a girl in the wheelchair and I felt really bad for her. She could not even see the demonstration that was going on because the tables were too high. I talked to her a bit and I didn't really go into her disability or how she feels about it, I just helped her with the assignment. She didn't know what was going on. There needed to be a better way of facilitating. Nobody talked to her. I felt so bad. She was already apart from the other students and none of us were going there, which was amazing. I was just amazed. That was the worst thing I ever saw in a class. I felt so bad, but I helped her. I'm sure every classroom is different but it was embarrassing for her not really knowing what was going on, and how many times has that happened, how many classrooms? Everything was so narrow for us, so imagine someone in a wheelchair in there.

During this experience I actually expected myself to be able to engage in conversation with students more easily, but it was actually pretty hard. I didn't know what to start with. I didn't know what to say to them and I think that's mostly because I didn't know them at all. When you start knowing people, you know what they're interested in and create better dialogue that way. I was afraid. I was really afraid, intimidated by the classroom when I first went there, but the students, the kids started doing work and we started socializing with them and stuff, and all my fears went 'swoosh.' It's not that bad, they aren't these big scary high school kids. They're all kind of small and pretty nice.

I guess I expected it to be quite intimidating an experience and really crazy and chaotic and actually it was, but I felt when I was there, it was good chaos, they were doing stuff. I always thought, '*You know, when that happens, how am I going to get control back?*'

But there's some good methods used there that I picked up. I just hope that because of my age that they'll take me seriously.

It's my biggest fear, that I'll go into a class and they'll say, "You're not much older than me! Who are you to tell me what to do?"

We had a presentation last week in the large lecture hall. Oh man! It was horrible. Everybody left just devastated. It involved students and teachers from a high school. Those kids came in more like teachers and a lot of people felt like they were talking down to us. They focused too much on appearance. How is that going to affect our teaching? Is our teaching going to be more effective if we dress properly or if we look proper? I don't think so. You know, they're saying we should wear business attire. We thought it was very Eurocentric. They were all whites and most of them are all, well I guess, they came from upper-class families. Three students seemed to be keeners in the class, where as we would have liked some input on how to deal with the hard kids and see what they expect from us. I mean, we know how to deal with the girls and the boys that are going to be good. We need to know how to deal with those that are going to be a problem. I think it was a general consensus that nobody really liked it. We really didn't get anything from it, just feeling bad about ourselves and that we're not good enough.

The two or three days that followed, we were all uneasy, and it would come up in general conversation in class, and someone would say something that related to the presentation. It happened in every class. In some classes, the instructors asked what we thought. We were trying to be nice, but after letting it sink in, it really wasn't a very good experience for me. I didn't like it at all. Nobody really did. They had ten do's and ten don'ts. So the ten don'ts: don't be lazy; don't be late; or unorganized; don't be inconsistent; don't pretend to be your student's friend or their age, which really blew us away. Why would we pretend to be their friends? We're not supposed to be friends with them. Don't take an unreasonable amount of time to mark, which made sense. Don't use sarcasm; don't give too much homework; don't say, "Just because;" don't think everyone loves and understands the subject you are teaching; don't bring emotional baggage or use pressure or intimidation.

There were two teachers at the presentation. One seemed sort of artsy, she teaches English, and the other said, "I don't tell my students anything about my personal life. I don't tell them my first name, I don't tell them if I am married, if I have kids, where I live, anything, they don't know anything about me, and that's the way it is." She was like the school master type. It was scary.

She was really scary and they actually like that type of person! They've been conditioned to it since Grade 1, so it works for them, but how many of us are going to be in schools like that?

I thought it was ridiculous. Sometimes the best way to get to know people is to be friendly and honest. Students need to know you are human too. It is respect both ways; we're all people. If you are just going to be a drill sergeant, I don't know. The dos were: Be energetic and dynamic; give encouragement; be prepared; be friendly and approachable. OK. For appearance, look put together; admit when you're wrong; have a sense of humour; earn respect; be adaptable; care and show it; be passionate, which is kind of contradictory. They went off on a big long tangent on how important it is that we look professional. First impressions and if you come in looking any less they won't take you seriously, blah, blah, blah. It was just amazing. The way they were talking to us, putting us in our place, they were telling us what to do when they should have been giving us suggestions rather than do this, do that, and don't do that. But they were really articulate. They were standing up there giving us a presentation and it was way better than any presentation I could possibly do in my life. If I could do half as good as these kids are doing! It was intimidating, the way they could stand up in front of this university group, no matter how many people were there.

Well, I went out shopping. Even before that presentation, our instructors were saying it's really important that you look professional. This is really tough for me because I'm an art person and my art teachers didn't look professional, they sort of did, but not really. I mean, you always just knew who the art teacher was. It's totally different being a math teacher or an English teacher which would make a little bit more sense dressing up. I bought a pair of shoes because I've got runners, and leather boots, and stuff like that. I went to Value Village and The Salvation Army. I have a few friends that have gotten too big for their clothes, they gave me some blouses and a button-up shirt, and then I had to go bra shopping which I thought, '*Oh great, this is going to be fun!*' I hate shopping, but you have to wear a bra under a white shirt. I bought a jacket, an overcoat jacket, a couple of skirts, so that was fine. I already have some black skirts that look good, but I got some colourful skirts and different ones. Everyone's going shopping, unless they've already got professional clothes. But what if you don't want to? Can't you just be yourself? No, they're looking for drone teachers. I'm in transition I guess. I'm trying to be myself but it's hard to mix the two. I'm realizing how public we are in a teaching position. I have to go get some new clothes and there's nothing wrong with that, but I'll get clothes that I can wear, and that are not promoting a certain kind of person, but clothes that reflect me.

We had another field visit, and at that school, everybody, the teachers, the principal, the students, they were all in black, gray or white. I just felt like I was going to a residential school or something. I don't think it's a very good example of what we'll experience as teachers. It might be a good example for people who are just going to those schools but not many will have that option. Going there made me realize that those people are already conditioned to certain behaviours, so you're not going to see them do anything else. I felt there weren't very many minorities, and there weren't that many lower-class people in either school on our field visits. It would be totally different if we were to actually go to a school downtown, which I think we would totally gain something from. It would be much more beneficial. I've been thinking, maybe I should actually write them a letter and say that next year I'd suggest a presentation by members from three different schools. What about the troubled students, what do they have to say?

It will be interesting when we all get back after our short practicum and share our experiences. I'm actually fearing being placed in one school. I just don't want to be there. But I figure, if I end up getting placed there, it'll be a good challenge and maybe it'll breakdown whatever it is that is making me not want to be there. The practicum is coming so soon. I guess I'm still worried mostly about the practicum, and the workload. I'm afraid if I do my practicum at that school, I'll make all sorts of mistakes and what if I really screw up? Then I'll have to leave home. I'll have to move somewhere else.

I've always been an activist-type person

The first day of the short practicum was overwhelming. This was my experience: As soon as I walked in the door the teachers were like, 'You are going to be doing this, and this is what you are going to do, to find this you go here and blah, blah, blah, blah.' In the end I just felt like it all went over my head. It was fine once we started to get to know each other. I was split between two teachers and I went between two classes, spending two classes with one and two classes with the other, no break between. I really liked it because they were two completely different teachers from each other and I got to see their different ways of doing things.

I'm not sure if I had Grade 8, but I know I had Grade 9, 10, 11, 12. One of the classes was a Grade 11/12 3-dimensional art class, very self-directed, and the kids were there because they wanted to be there. They were coming up with very creative things. It was pretty open and they used various media. The other class was where they just stuck all the students that they couldn't find a place for. It was all Grade 10's. The class consisted of mostly special needs students and behavioural problem students. It was most teachers' worst nightmare, but they weren't that bad. All kids aren't that bad. It was pretty crazy. I ended up teaching that class for the full week so I learned a lot from doing it. I don't know if they had as much fun as me! I was told by the faculty advisor after she had observed a few classes that last year a student-teacher failed because she couldn't handle a class like that. She freaked out and just ran off crying.

The only thing that didn't work for me was having to overcome the students' idea that I'm not their teacher. I diffused the situation by not letting them convince me that I don't have the power of the teacher, cause I did really, that's why I was there, more of a sub than a student. That was the only thing that kept me going over their malicious attacks within the classroom structure. They were just testing anyway. I don't start yelling or raising my voice. I tried to keep it short and sweet.

One of the biggest things I learned was that I can't expect or assume my students can read. I was trying to get them to be engaged by reading, but a few of them had a really hard time. This poor kid was stuttering, and I thought, '*Oh no! I shouldn't have done that.*'

The short practicum made me think, maybe I won't teach full-time. I would not have so many time management problems and more time for myself, and a better balance. A typical schedule only has one spare block, but I didn't really have a spare block when I was observing and I was running around and I couldn't do that all the time. My sponsor teacher taught four blocks, and next term she's doing two. I don't know how she did it. She's got kids. I wouldn't want to have kids and teach full time, it just isn't going to happen! It's really hard to teach full-time in art. There is only one full-time art teacher in the district; the rest are sporadic, getting an art course here and there, so I have a feeling it will work out that way. I would prefer to stick with art, only if I'm able to teach it the way I want to, because it is most important to me to try to teach a lot of subjects through art. I've considered teaching art history and even social studies and English because they all link to art. Looking back, I thought teaching was a lot harder, to stand up in front of the classroom. Maybe it's because the class I had seemed so young, it was very comfortable for me. I also didn't realize that students are so used to having a power structure, even the ones that challenge it.

It was really hard in one of the art classes to hear that the students were not going to be able to do a project if they didn't pay their fee, which was an extra fee the school was not supposed to have, but the teacher decided to put it in place. She said that their artwork, which was clay, would be recycled when they were done if they didn't pay. I was really concerned about it. I mentioned it a few times and I think that really affected the teacher, who decided in the end to drop the fee. Only 5 of 30 students paid.

I said, "How are they going to be motivated to do the project if it's just going to be destroyed in the end and what do you guys do for students who can't afford to pay this extra fee?"

And the response was there's nothing they could do. In the end she decided that because they had a little bit of extra overhead from last year, she would put that aside. She used it as a power thing over them to pay if they could, but I think at an earlier point she should have mentioned, if you can't pay, you get to keep it anyways. I saw a lot of them just not doing it because it was going to be destroyed and I couldn't tell them that she changed her mind. That was her decision.

I just said, "Come on, do a good job."

I wouldn't do that to students. I would find some way to fundraise or something because I saw how it affected them. There were a lot of little things, like in the photography class, the teacher would make them draw cameras instead of taking pictures, if they couldn't afford the film and developer and stuff. So it was absolutely ridiculous. It was such old school stuff. It is very discouraging when you're actually out there, and people start hating you for stepping on their toes all the time. I felt like I couldn't say anything during some conversations. I do feel that we should have had a little more time to sit and observe and not have to worry about doing things and writing things, and juggling a million things at once, which is what ended up happening. It's frustrating though because I have so many ideas of where I should be and the things I should change. There's so much I want to do in life. I guess I've always been an activist-type person. I want to do things but I feel like there's a barrier between knowing it all and doing it all, and I don't know how to get between the two.

I found myself in a place I visited often

I've been thinking about the role of the student in the role of the teacher. This is probably the last time I'm going to be able to be the student. I'll probably go to school again but not like this. I see myself as equal to all around me, staff, students, administrators. I reluctantly use my power, position, and authority as the teacher to meet the requirements of the Ministry of Education. I try to fit in, blend in, until I can have the freedom of my own class where things will be different, where I will work towards creating a learning environment where there is less authority and more learning. But I feel, know and internalize the struggle. To undo what has been done, the conditioning of the students, and myself in my K-12 education and in my postsecondary and teacher education, and in society as a whole, is going to be the biggest struggle ever. I feel like I work alone, like I am trying to put out a grass fire in the field with the wind working against me in every direction.

I see being an artist coming out more in the role I play of being a teacher than student. I'm coming from an academic perspective, not getting anything done, and even the things I am getting done aren't of great quality, like my ceramics. I'm working more textually than visually lately. My hands and body feel so distant from creation. My role as an artist has transformed from what it was, or more like, the role has evolved in a way. It was about creation before and it moved towards sending a message, but that message I know did not reach many, so now teaching has become my paintbrush and it paints the faces of hopefully many more warriors than it would have on the canvas.

Sometimes what I read or learn not only makes sense but really excites me and relates to my own life, the life of others around me and my beliefs about what education should be about. For the most part, I embody the wonderful teaching strategies and ideas that pop up along the way. Strategies and ideas that are fun, inclusive, inspiring, engaging and educational. Classes on multiculturalism or antiracism, or gender roles and stuff like that really spark my thinking. With any of these issues, you want to be ethical and moral, but you don't want to impose it on other people, so if you promote multiculturalism and the acceptance of other people, and some cultures don't accept people who are gay, what then?

Being First Nations, these issues are very important and the reason why I'm here. I saw a need for it and felt a need for it. In my family, we were distanced from the negative, the downside of First Nations life. We didn't live on the reserve. We didn't develop the social language. I think it impaired our social abilities at first and it took a long time to regain that. We also didn't get the mainstream culture. We didn't have TV, and I think that really helped finding out who we are. These social issues have me thinking outside of my perspective, and also thinking of the struggles between social issues. Sometimes the questions seem to have obvious answers but when we dig deeper, consider it from a different point of view, not just ethnicity, class, religion, but many different points of view, the answer becomes questionable, the question needs definition or more questioning. It's a complex system we are entering into. The biggest question I have is, as secondary school educators teaching adolescents, will it be too much for them to handle or to comprehend if I bring up these questions? Of course, the easy answer is no, but in reality they need a lot more information, knowledge, experience and background in order to understand, not to mention tackle such questions. There are a lot of inequalities that need to be addressed and rectified in the world. Much of it is hidden beneath the surface, in cracks and corners.

I remember specific moments in the school where I was doing my practicum. I had strong feelings throughout my mind and body. They were like flashbacks but stronger. I spent a lot of time skipping school in the ninth and tenth grade, where I skipped classes to see friends at the school I was doing my practicum in. I was there a lot, had many experiences from the hallways, bathrooms, smoke pit, schoolyard, and surrounding areas. Being back there brought back many of the feelings I experienced in that space. It was quite an embodying experience that really shook me actually. I can't explain exactly how it felt or what it did to me, but it really did affect me. I guess it brought me back to the level of understanding the youth in the class, understanding the things that they value and struggle with in their position, in their personal lives. The other thing I noticed was their attire. Many of them were wearing clothes much like I remember wearing. The shirts from bands that I remember being in love with while I went to school and now even. I guess they are timeless legends and their music just relates to the school experience for adolescents.

I think being home for the short practicum was very important. The land and objects hold memories of past experiences and feelings. They talk to you in a way. It seems everyone has a place they go to unwind and find their center. You might question why this place does that for you. Is it the environment? Is it a memory or ritual which brings you back to that place? When I went on my practicum, I took a weekend to get back to my roots, to unwind. I found myself in a place I visited often in the past. But this time it was different, it was a different season with different smells, appearance, and feel. I hadn't been to this place in a long while, six years or so. It was much like the flashbacks I felt in the school, but deeper. It brought me back to a very calm place, into a spiritual dialogue with the world and myself. The environment spoke to me, not so much spoke, but showed me what I had been missing. The season was late autumn, calm, still, crisp and fresh. It showed me what I already knew in my head but it showed my body. My body needed to remember and feel that space so it could find its way back. I often knew in my mind and body that I needed to be there. I guess my mind and body had forgotten exactly what and where that place was, how it should feel, and how to get there. So now it remembers. I go there daily, hourly even, because I have to.

I just swallow hard

While on the short practicum, I felt invisible to some people and visible to others. It seemed like some people hardly acknowledged my presence while others were very aware and treated me almost as equal. Some people were completely not acknowledging my existence, maybe they mistook me for a student or maybe they didn't want to, maybe not knowing what to say. So a few people were friendly, and I got into a couple of conversations with a few other people but I stuck to my teacher and to a couple of other practicum students who were there. Sometimes during practicum, I felt like I wasn't listened to or that I should be silent in order to maintain my status. Mostly I feel oppressed or marginalized due to my youthful appearance. Most people say something about my age even if they don't realize it. I feel like I am subject to a lot of political debates and structures. I also notice a hierarchy of politics within the school during practicum.

Not having the acknowledgement of other teachers was weird. In the staff room, I felt like I was eavesdropping during conversations. I could've jumped into the conversations but I didn't want to because I didn't want to say anything out of place and they would probably think, '*You don't know the half of it!*'

And I just felt like an outsider. I didn't really feel any extremely welcoming moments, except with my first sponsor teacher, she was absolutely amazing, very helpful. And I think she's probably the reason that I stayed there and why I'm going to be able to deal with the next semester, because I was able to talk to her once in a while and say, "This is what's going on." The rest of them are really busy and in their own little worlds. I'm not too sure what may have been the problem, negativity, not quite negative but, they're kind of standoffish and that may have been the problem. They had problems before with student-teachers and maybe they don't say anything around them because they may say something to the wrong people or who knows. I'm sure I would have been received totally different at the other school, the one I graduated from. Everyone would have been friendly, 'Oh hey, you're back. It's great to see you.' And people who didn't know me, they would probably introduce themselves, and here, if staff walk down the hallway, they would probably just walk right by parents.

I am a very quiet, in my own world person, so maybe it's good for me. I don't know. I would rather have the family environment the other school has. I think it adds to the experience. When you are in the staff room and you are having a good conversation with people and you go to class and then you start teaching and you're still in that mood. But when you go to your staff room and you're sitting there by yourself and eating lunch, and you're looking over things that you've got to do and go to the classroom and you're still on mind-time, there's no real slowing down, no relief time.

On practicum, I tried to be neutral, but I tried to influence things once in a while. I think the practicum is kind of like a long-term interview to find out what kind of person I really am and if I'm the kind of person they really want there, because if they want people who will do things differently, I can do that. But I didn't want to do something and then be kicked out of there. I have strong beliefs about the world, about a lot of things, and I'm the kind of person who usually gets up and starts saying something, to say what I think. I'll take whatever consequences even if I have to lose my job sometimes. I just can't do it now, it is too important to get through this program and also not to gain too many enemies. It depends on the people who are around, who I'm with, if they'll receive me graciously or not. Some people would be totally offended and would hold a grudge forever.

Being part of a minority race within education, not to mention Canada, puts me at some advantage as the education system seeks more diversity in its staffing. I think being female is advantageous because students are often more willing to open up to female teachers than male, but that is just an assumption on my part, males may feel more comfortable opening up to male role models. As I am part of the lower class, I have totally different views about many things. I notice middle and high class people take their financial stability for granted and they assume that anyone can afford the little things. I find I don't have the luxury of buying new clothes, wonderful school supplies or going out for lunch, dinners, drinks or other extracurricular experiences. I noticed that in my social issues class everyone seemed to assume that the people in the class were middle class or better, and heterosexual. They often saw people of different races as representatives of that race and they had a hard time commenting on issues of race when that person was present.

I have always been the type of person who enjoys solitude and seeks it often. But lately, throughout this first semester at university, I feel very isolated. The university is large but it seems that everyone is confined to their quarters on campus as well as within the faculty. Science people never mingle with art people and so on. Outside of university, I have very little time to become involved in anything else. My daily routine consists of waking up, eating, if I have time, saying hello to my boyfriend online, then heading out the door to the bus, waiting for the bus and on the bus there is no interaction, people read, sleep, talk on cell phones and listen to music. I get off the bus and it's the same thing, walking in crowds without any conversation or interaction. I get to class and have a few minutes to chat sometimes. After class it's time for homework, or eats. I went out a couple of times with students from the cohort, but then it is back to homework. My roommates are not great company so I shut my door. Sometimes, I don't want to get up and out of bed, especially when my body feels very negatively towards something. I just swallow hard, especially if it seems I am the only one having the problem. I sometimes try to keep my distance from the other students so they don't influence my decisions and assignments too much, or so that they don't take too much of mine. Sometimes it is good to gain from their ideas too. I don't really feel like a teacher. I feel more like a coordinator than a teacher. I feel that a teacher is sometimes too strong of a word for how I would like to run the classroom. I would prefer to be more in a coordinator or in a participant-type role. I mostly fear how my sponsor teacher will receive me and my teaching methods and strategies on the long practicum. She is very strict, an old school 'my way or no way' type person. She said she acknowledges that we will have different teaching styles and that will be OK, but I fear she has no idea how different we really are and I hope that doesn't interfere with my experience and practicum, or my life too much.

Many of the schools in the school district I'm entering are resistant to accepting student-teachers. The teacher that finally decided to take me after the short practicum was very resistant to having a student-teacher come in. She seemed resistant towards me until one day she got to know me on a more personal level. I wrote an introductory letter so that she could relate to me better. But my head and body are resistant towards the long practicum. Fear or something is setting in but I won't let it take over. I have the same feelings toward this family reunion t-shirt I am supposed to have designed by now. Too much pressure. I just don't feel I can do it. The fact of the matter is that I just have to do it, just do it!

I want to try new things and experiment

I'm kind of afraid of how things will go with the teacher because I've been sending e-mails back and forth and she seems to have a lack of confidence in my abilities I guess. I sent her an e-mail with some ideas for my first week, but she sent me an e-mail saying that it was too much classroom management to start with, and it is only one class! So I emailed her back, writing, 'Oh, okay.' I understand she has experience and all that; I was just trying to start with something a little easy. I put it nicely, but I was worried that she lacked confidence in me. I also said that there would be a time where I wanted to try new things and experiment and stuff. She e-mailed me back and said basically that I won't do anything that she hasn't seen before. I was just like, 'Wow! Okay.' I've already had a couple things rejected and if I do too many it's a lot of wasted work. I bit my tongue and thought I had better just leave it at that. But I was already thinking, it's not about what she's seen before, it's about me. I'm paying to be there and they need to know that. I don't know, it's got to be sort of a power thing, and that will be the hardest thing to get over.

For the long practicum, I'm working with the Grade 8's because they always have sort of a book of things that they cover. I'm just going to jump into it. All these things I've been thinking about are coming into my dreams lately, like getting to sleep, getting to the class on time, and the classroom, thinking, *'What am I going to do? How am I going to make these kids listen?'* And then, I keep thinking, *'I should have pushed, really pushed to go to the other school.'* There's less personal interaction in this school amongst the teachers and amongst the teachers and students. But I would be too afraid of it being a conflict of interest, where people see my request as a negative thing because the only other option would be going to the other school with the same art teacher that I used to have when I was a student, and we're already sort of friends. I'm afraid of being too much of an easy-going pushover that the students will take advantage of me. I just don't know if I can actually pull off being a tough me. I can't wait until it is over.

Right now everyone in the cohort is just fending for themselves and dealing with their own problems because everyone has different teachers. There are a few things that we do talk about. We talk about teachers and we discuss problems and issues, and what we are each doing. I would consider teaching in other places and see what it is like because I have a feeling there might be a place with better things. But then, maybe this is the best it gets. When I'm done, I'm going to take a year. I'm hoping not to get a full-time job now. I would like to be TOC'ing.[1] I want to deinstitutionalize myself! I feel like I'm a total foreigner from all these kids in the class because I have all this knowledge I want to give them but they're not going to understand me at all. I need to understand them. So I think I need to tone it down a little. I learned a lot about the restraints that teachers

---

[1] The term 'TOC' refers to teacher on call.

have and things they can't do, and the powerlessness they have in the classroom because overall, government has power.

My head is just going a million miles a minute. What do I do, what do I need, I'm up all night, I don't want to be up all night, I just can't sleep. I actually got some sleeping pills from my doctor. I think it's just that my sleeping schedule from the holidays is totally messed up. I think my biggest fear is that it's not going to work out between me and the teacher and then I don't know. I'm just wondering if I will give up because of too much stress, or if I just can't do it anymore, or it's not worth it, or something like that. I hope the long practicum will just fly by. I just want to get it over with. It was scary, that first week of the short practicum. I was all over the place and felt like my head was chopped off for just one class and I'm going to have three later on, and I'm thinking that's a lot of work. I'm wondering how the students are going react to me after being in the classroom and telling them what to do. Are they going to listen or are they going to do a half-assed job or what? And if I can't get these kids to do their work then what good am I as a teacher? I just don't know what I'm going to do on the practicum and how I'm going to get them interested in art when they don't have any supplies.

I had to be a root of care to the tree of unhappiness that lived in the classroom

My long practicum was physically and emotionally draining but encompassed with rewards and lessons throughout. I found moments where my point of view and ideas on teaching, school or students differed from my sponsor teachers. I need to work on how I approach such situations. I need to be more cautious so as not to seem argumentative, I need to avoid conflict, and offending those involved. I learned that I am strong, I can overcome any obstacle and I want to give as much as I can.

I was successful with classroom management. Most of the students respected me and behaved appropriately. My most successful lesson was on the mandala because the imagery and statements turned out very strong for each individual in the class. I also felt quite positive about having a guest speaker and artist come in to diffuse stereotypes with knowledge and lived experiences for the students to learn from. I had a hard time when students expressed negative attitudes towards lessons. I took that personally. It's like getting a bad review on an artwork that you have invested a lot into, or a bad grade on a paper that you put a lot of time into and feel strongly about. Trying to get through to some students was frustrating as well. I also struggled in dealing with the sponsor teacher always being there, sticking out like a sore thumb, constantly jumping into situations and taking over as she pleased. It was hard trying to satisfy her standards. There was a need for space and distance from the sponsor teacher that I was unable to maintain under the circumstances. Later in the practicum, I struggled with morning sickness throughout the day. I realized that good health and energy is crucial in teaching to my fullest abilities. It takes a lot of energy to teach and organization is essential for survival.

My life contrasted greatly with many of the students' lives as well as the sponsor teachers' lives. My life has many complexities and difficulties that many of the students and teachers could never really understand. This made it hard at times for the students and teachers to understand me and for me to accept their lives and attitudes without being judgmental. Although, in some cases, it brought my sponsor teacher or faculty advisor and me closer together, bonding, as you could put it. When I became pregnant, I did not feel comfortable telling my sponsor teacher or the school district for fear of judgment or jeopardizing chances at obtaining a job. It was difficult hiding the fact and dealing with its effects on my teaching. I would have liked to be more honest in order to have their support and understanding along the way.

On another note, private lives affected my practicum experience, and I did not expect to have to deal so much with the private lives of the people involved. My sponsor teacher regularly delved into her private matters, using me as a support system and friend, asking for advice and thoughts about situations I personally did not feel I should venture into. My faculty advisor also had many personal matters and health issues throughout the practicum to which I had to be sensitive to, work around and deal with. I was previously under the impression that our relationships were supposed to be strictly professional but they ended up becoming quite personal and in so doing, it was hard to tell where I might cross lines in our relationships. I felt like I had to be a root of care to the tree of unhappiness that lived in the classroom.

I felt a neighbouring teacher showed the most care towards both the students and me. This was where I turned to for help and recluse throughout my practicum. The care in my own classroom, especially from my sponsor teacher, seemed limited and superficial but it did exist. My sponsor teacher, faculty advisor and fellow teachers were excellent mentors in my teaching. They provided me with a variety of techniques and tips that came from many valuable years of experience. My mother was also a great mentor, providing me with insight, knowledge, skills and supports that she had gained from her experiences working in elementary schools.

It was both more and less work than I had anticipated. It seemed to take up every minute of time I had, plus some! I found myself doing things I had not anticipated would take so long, such as gathering resources and preparing for demonstrations. I spent less and less time on lesson plans and learned to take things as they come. Looking back, I would have planned more self-directed projects for the students to explore their own interests and artistic abilities. I would have also put more effort into getting to know the other teachers and participating in more school-wide events.

When I was feeling ill, drained both physically and mentally, and especially when the students seemed so disinterested, I questioned if this was really for me. I kept thinking of how much I would rather just be working in a studio doing what I love to do. I also thought about all the other jobs that I am already qualified to do that probably pay about the same or more and the workload is much less. In the end, I practiced discipline knowing I would regret making such decisions in the long run. The practicum was tough, and so it should be, but I had to focus on the fact that it would get easier and there is light at the end of the tunnel. I had many reasons for choosing this path, and to jump off it because it got a little rocky would surely prove to be a mistake. Other things that helped keep me on track were the Grade 8 students' passion, energy and creativity. I also had my family and friends supporting and encouraging me, but not pressuring me.

I hope to open their eyes

Now that I'm done, I feel relieved, excited to enter the workforce and a bit nervous about the first day back. I'll probably be alone and a little rusty. I wonder how the students will receive me, and will they behave? How will the staff receive me? What classes will I have to TOC for? Will I know the material? How well can I improvise if needed?

The last day I attended classes I remember thinking, I was glad that there was only one week left but also overwhelmed with the amount of homework and pressure. Since I ended up in the hospital for the final week due to my pregnancy, it took me an extra couple of weeks to finish the final classes while on bed-rest. The instructors were somewhat accommodating to my circumstance but in some ways, they really could not have understood the severity of the situation. It was hard to concentrate and perform the tasks needed. In the end, it was hoop jumping.

As a teacher, I am still young and energetic, full of great ideas and willing to take risks both in the classroom, as well as with administration and staff. I am strong and soft when needed. I think that my desire to create change and willingness to challenge the system when needed could make or break me throughout my career. I figure I will try to use good judgment as to when and where to exercise my freedom of speech and power, when to push and when to flow. As long as I stay true to what I believe I will be okay with the results of my actions, whatever they may be. I am a visionary with not enough time, money, space, energy or material to complete my ideas. This has been my artist self since I can remember, but I am determined and when inspired, I do manage to complete some of my artwork. I am always seeking answers and driven to succeed. Beyond that, I am driven to learn, about EVERYTHING. I'm not looking at knowledge as power but knowledge for understanding and informing decisions within myself, my life, and for passing on such knowledge. I want each student to grow as opposed to achieve. I hope to open their eyes rather than tell them what to see and do. I view teaching as much more than passing on information and skills. I see it as so much more, but at the same time I feel like teachers are caged birds held back by society. This will never change. So when we get the opportunity to sneak out of the cage once in a while, why not take it, but be wary of the cats waiting for just the right moment to pounce.

UNCERTAINTY:
NATHALIE'S STORY

I have no real expectations of this program

I have a background in art. My ideas for my work come from what I observe in my environment. When I finished my art degree, I started exhibiting. I began pushing myself because the program has a great opportunity in that when you graduate, you put on an entire show in a gallery. You have to go from start to finish and work it out. It was wonderful. After I graduated, that show went to Edmonton, Regina and to other places. It was a really great experience, but I feel like I left that life. It's been on pause for three years.

My first experience teaching was with ESL, Grades 1 to 9, and I loved it, but I was really reluctant to go towards teaching because everyone in my family is a teacher – grandma, mom, auntie. My grandma was a one-room schoolteacher on the Prairies, teaching Grades 1 to 12. I wasn't sure about teaching. The weight of the whole commitment scared me. Do I want to sign up for a 30-year plan? Because that's what everyone in my family has done. But after the ESL experience, which was just amazing, I thought I really do enjoy this.

I only moved to the city a month before the program started, so I had to get a place to live. I don't really feel like I have a social network yet, but that will come. I've been feeling really depressed, and I think it's because I am still in transition. I have no real expectations of this program. I think in some ways that is working to my advantage because I don't really have any room for disappointment. Still it's been very hard coming back. I get emotional even talking about it.

I thought it would be great if I could be creating things while teaching, and combining those two realms of my past. And even today, I'm realizing this is good, I've made a good choice, I mean, it is pretty stressful. We were talking this morning, holy crow, it's only been three weeks but it feels like a year. When I talk to people, they seem more excited than I am, like my family or friends, they're just so excited. *'Well,'* I thought, *'I'll go and see what it is like.'* And even the first day, I wasn't definite. But this is it. I'm pretty certain I'll finish the program, it's only a year. It's such a great opportunity and it will give me so much. I think what always worried me is that I didn't know what kind of teacher I wanted to be. I don't want to be like the memories I have of the authority figure at the front. That memory put me off teaching for a while. Seeing as I grew up in a house full of teachers, I'm very familiar with the strict, stern voice. My mom totally has a teacher voice and when it comes out you know you're in trouble.

I want to be a teacher who is open, available, involved, a good listener, can laugh at oneself, who is fun, open to change, someone who can learn from others, who takes risks, who experiments, explores and evolves. I feel I'm back in the educational system as the student even though we are training to be teachers. Teaching ESL taught me the stresses of being a teacher. You ask yourself, *'What am I doing tomorrow? What materials am I bringing? What are the students going to be doing? What are the objectives?'* But those worries aren't present for me at this point. This program asks you to get back into a scholarly mindset where you have to sit down and write an essay response to a reading. So at this point in the program I really don't feel like a teacher. Although even when I was teaching, I'm not sure if I felt like one. When I was teaching in the classroom and responsible for curriculum and all that stuff, I didn't feel that it was my room, even though I often refer to them as my kids. It was our room. So I come to this program from that perspective.

We're training to be art teachers and it's really great that the professors are emphasizing the fact we need to be continually working on our art while we are in the program. A lot of the people in my cohort know each other. I don't know if they are friends but some went through art training together. I talked to another girl last night who said when she walked in on the first day, she looked around and she thought she was in the wrong place because everyone seemed to know each other. She actually left and then checked the door, as if to say, *'No this is it,'* and went back in. I am just amazed that people have spouses or families and are doing this program. I was thinking about it, and maybe because I don't have a social network yet, I have all the time in the world to do this, but I'm feeling pretty consumed by it already. This is all I'm doing on weekends. I was here all Saturday.

We were on a field visit to a school last week, and I know our instructors talk a lot about Code 5, which says we can't talk about other teachers, but I felt like I was really in the way as an observer and it made me so uncomfortable. The room was small, but it felt even smaller because of the atmosphere. After that experience, I just thought this is not for me, unless I can reinvent this entire profession, this is not for me. It was my first time back to a high school art classroom in ten years, so there's been a big gap. I just felt terrible. I didn't want to walk around and interact with the students because of the atmosphere conveyed, and even if it's not directly articulated, it is in the air. I felt very intrusive, but the saving grace was there was another situation where I walked into the room and the room embraced me. It seemed bigger and everyone was smiling. I was included in the lesson and encouraged to use materials, sit down, have a chair, and it was great. I feel so sensitive right now, this emotional roller coaster, within two or three hours of seeing the classrooms, we were discussing our experience and no one really seemed to say what I just said. I think because I'm self-critical and constantly analyzing myself, I have the chance to grow into something, something really great and I hope that happens because it could go the other way and it could cave in and everything could come crashing down. Sometimes I wonder if it's just my nature. I'm constantly questioning myself. I guess we are our biggest critic. I really hope that when I come out of this, I'm confident, I know what is expected for each grade level, and I really want to stay informed. I just hope that once I'm comfortable with set criteria then I can really explore and have fun with what I'm doing.

Looking ahead, I'm concerned about the practicum. I think it's my fear of being in front of an audience. I've heard that it's much easier to stand in front of students on the practicum than when you're in front of your cohort peers. I hope that is true. The whole 'everyone look at me I'm going to say something,' that makes me nervous.

She wants to be the 'cool teacher'

We had a lecture with three high school students and three teachers, and it was a hard lecture for me. I thought the point of view they presented was so narrow. The students were all white, high achievers, excelling in math and French. It was interesting to me, when we got into our cohort, none of that was addressed. I was still processing what I had just seen, so I didn't bring any of this up in class and it was just kind of skipped. I'm thinking of doing a response in my visual journal. I don't know if it was what they were actually saying or how they were presenting the information. It came across as if teachers aesthetically present themselves in a certain way, they'll be fine. It's almost like saying, *'OK, if you spend all this money and buy all new clothes and you are hip and trendy, then you will be accepted, no problem, and the kids will like you. Providing you don't show your thong or wear a velour tracksuit.'* This is all coming from the high school kids! Recently we had been talking about wardrobe and presenting the teacher image as a cohort. There were a couple of exercises where we had to come to school dressed like an art teacher and then had pictures taken of us. I wanted to make a paper doll, just to give myself some different options for costumes and see 2-dimensionally what is really going on with that kind of peer pressure as the teacher to fit in. It was just bizarre. Of course, I know some stuff is inappropriate even just in a professional definition; obviously, I can't wear jeans or sneakers. That's just common sense, but the way it came out at the lecture, I feel I have to portray this really fashionable person. It seemed a lot about income and displaying your income through your dress and that is how you are going to get respect, and I thought that doesn't make any sense.

When I think about the teachers I had, I remember my two art teachers, what they wore. One lady was very hippy, lots of floral and wide muu-muu style stuff, and lots of wood beads and big hair. And the man, this British guy, would always wear cords and a collared shirt, so that was his uniform. In some ways I want to reinvent myself in this role. So I thought maybe before I go through the anxiety of standing up in something that doesn't feel right, maybe I should experiment with that on paper. You have to be presentable and businesslike and you do have to be different than the kids. I don't think you necessarily have to spend a lot of money or have to change everything; maybe you could wear a blazer with the sneakers, and just find some give-and-take. It really got me thinking in the morning as to why I'm choosing certain articles, that there is a conscious decision I make every morning and I thought it was a good exercise to get me thinking about the teacher image. I really had to think a lot more. I wore my glasses because I thought it gave me a more librarian look. So I've just been thinking about that in terms of imagery. I don't know. I couldn't wear jeans and I couldn't wear a sleeveless shirt and things that were too short, obviously you can't show midriff at all and you can't show chest, even a bare arm is kind of bad. No jewellery, no hair accessories, unless you are very modest, like a black elastic or white elastic for your hair, or something that blends in and no nail polish and stuff. It's very laid out as to what is acceptable. So I think I will buy some key pieces.

Today we just had a meeting about our short practicum, and things to do and not to do. I really want to seem engaged, but not intrusive. I'll probably lay low for a bit and then work my way around, that's how I'm comfortable. I don't like barging in and saying, "What are you doing?" I'd rather connect through osmosis, slowly blend in. I'm still pretty nervous about the practicum. I feel like the short practicum is looming. I'm getting a lot of questions from family, like where are you going, so it's adding a little bit to my anxiousness, and feeling the pressure of the clothing and that countdown to practicum. I have to go out to Value Village and Winners and try to find some good deals. I overheard this girl in one of my classes talking about how she wants to be the 'cool teacher' and I thought, 'Oh.' She just kept going on about this pressure to be the cool teacher. I don't know. I don't really care if they think I'm cool. At the same time, I guess I do have some pressure. My initial reaction was to reject what she was saying but then maybe deep down, what she's saying isn't so foreign to me, and so I judged her, but at the same time, I'm thinking as I walk by shops, realizing I'm looking in the window thinking, *'Okay could I wear that? Could I pull that off?'* I feel like I need to do something to change, like I can't just go in and be me.

There are things coming up in other classes as well, discussing gender roles, the pressure of being a girl and you have to look put together. Even today in my cohort, one of the girls said to me, "Is that your natural hair color?"

And I said, "Yeah."

She said, "It's beautiful but you never style your hair, you should really try."

I come from a place where my mum doesn't do anything with her looks. She doesn't do up her hair, she's very natural, she doesn't wear makeup, and I only have brothers, so how am I supposed to learn how to style my hair? Then we go to this lecture about how teachers present themselves and I wonder, '*Is everyone feeling this pressure, or is it just me, or is it just girls or?*' We don't really think that what we look like influences our message, how people hear our message and hopefully no matter what, it's going to be the same message. Just recently, I started to become more aware of how that is not necessarily the case. My gender is a major issue for me during this process, being very aware of being female, and I don't know if that is something I'm always kind of dealing with or because all of the teachers in my family are women. I'm aware of the percentage of women in the program versus men. Yet it seemed to me, and I don't know if this is specific to my gender, but the qualities I have, sensitivity, things like this, aren't being valued. It seems like the program is very male oriented yet almost all of the members, the majority are female. So I didn't really understand that kind of weird dynamic, if it was problematic or not and if I was resisting or not. I'm not sure. I try to bring out masculine qualities in myself. I don't want to seem weak or girly.

In some ways the teacher role has become a domesticated one. When my grandma was a teacher, she lived in the one-room school all year, in the middle of the Prairies and in the winter, they were snowed in. She'd have her four kids including my mom and she would have to be very creative to survive, she'd have Spam and they'd have no running water, the well would freeze, they would have to go out and dig snow and boil the snow. So it was a very maternal role, constant, not only was she mother for her own kids, she was nurturing 25 other kids of all age levels in one room. She was just so resilient and resourceful, a tough lady and I think all the ladies in my family are like that, they are pretty tough. Teaching is so challenging. As a profession, it is occupied mostly by women and yet the qualities that women are encouraged to possess as people are not always welcome in our teachers. This is a problematic contradiction, one that I haven't sorted out yet.

I was so invisible

The short practicum wasn't so good. Actually it was terrible. I walked in the first day and we got a nice welcome by the vice principal, and a nice tour. There were eight of us, all girls from all different departments.

So we got the tour, everything was nice and then he said, "Okay we're to drop you off with your teachers."

We got to this English room, not an art room, and he said, "This is your student-teacher."

Classes had been in session for about 20 or 30 minutes, and the teacher said, "Oh what student-teacher?"

I was so invisible and no one was responsible for me and I had nothing. I had no space to be in. I totally knew this was going to happen because on Thursday before we went to school, I did some research on the Internet and looked up my sponsor teacher because I kept getting this information that we're not supposed to contact our sponsor teachers. And I was like, 'Hm ...'

I mean, my mom's a teacher and everybody in my family are teachers and they were saying what, we've never heard of that. They were saying, "I would be really upset if my student-teacher didn't contact me before they showed up." So I'm getting this information from my family, 'You have to contact them.' And from the program here, 'Don't contact them.' In the end I didn't contact him. I just did a little research on my own.

The vice principal says, "Okay here you go, sort it out between the two of you, didn't you get the memo?" And he leaves me there. I walk in and there's no extra chair, and I'm standing there, in front of a Grade 11 English class doing silent reading. The teacher didn't introduce me. And this is totally not his fault, because he didn't know he was getting a student! How come this guy didn't know anything about me?

So he's feeling the exact same way I'm feeling! He said, "Well I don't know what you want to do here, but what's your name and what are you all about."

"I'm training to be in art teacher."

"Oh! I'm not an art teacher."

"Oh, well, what do you teach?"

"English and photo."

"Oh yeah?"

"I wouldn't call it artistic because it is photo. I just picked it up and have been doing it for 'x' number of years." He uses the same handout every single year, he's never changed it. So, okay, I'll make the best of the situation.

He says, "Why don't you take a walk."

I thought, *'Take a walk, what you mean?'*

He added, "I don't know what you're doing here so why don't you just go for a walk."

So I went out, I left, and I'm in the halls, thinking, *'Okay don't get freaked out, this is fine, it's going to get better.'* For three days, he didn't introduce me. Nobody knew who I was. I kept asking him to introduce me, but he kept forgetting. I had no space. One day he left and didn't say goodbye and my stuff got locked in his office. I had to find a custodial worker, explain who I was, and they couldn't open his office because they'd never met me, so finally I got a substitute to open the door for me. The whole time the substitute is ranting and raving about how the school is a nightmare, he's been there for four days and there hasn't been a single lesson plan left for him and he's just up in arms about the whole thing. This goes on for four days, not being introduced, not being with an art teacher, having one block of photo, and spending the rest of the day in the art room with a substitute because the teacher was on conference leave. This was really uncomfortable. Every day I went home and cried. And I just felt like I wanted to interact with the kids, but didn't feel comfortable until they were familiar with why I was there, who I was, and that never got dealt with so I had to deal with it myself.

On the fourth day, I thought, '*Okay, I'm just going to go up to every group, and make my rounds, introduce myself and ask them who they are.*' And so I did that and I learned every single one of their names. I found out what they were working on. I found that they all hated that class. It was such a negative environment.

The fifth day, the Friday, I believe it was, I go to school, thinking, '*Okay, the first week is almost over, it's been hell, I'm so glad it's Friday.*' I go into the art room, and there is this blonde lady standing there and I introduced myself and she turns out to be the lady that has been on conference leave. She is one of the art teachers, there's another art teacher and so, there's three teachers in the art room, the English teacher who's photo part-time, and two other part-time art teachers. But with this setup, there's no way I could get an 80% class load with those teachers in those circumstances. Anyhow, the addition of this new woman on Friday was like a godsend. She's French-Canadian, and she just started praising the sky in French, going on about how I'm this gift from heaven. She's kind of like a renegade in the school.

I kept trying to get acquainted with the staff, so I went to the library to take out a book and the librarian told me I wasn't allowed, because I would steal it.

She said, "We have terrible problems with the student-teachers, they're always stealing the books! So if you want to take out a book, you have to get your sponsor teacher to come up with you and sign out the book for you."

I had to go back down to my sponsor teacher, explain this to him, and he replied, "That's crap." He writes out this note on a piece of paper, 'Let her take out the damn book!!!' And I have to take this note up there. I was so embarrassed. I just put a note away. I didn't throw it away, but I didn't give it to her because I was so embarrassed. I didn't even go back. It was so ridiculous!

That same day at lunch, I went to the cafeteria, and the lunch lady started yelling at me! She thought I was a student and she yelled, "Hurry it up, you're holding up the whole line!" She was really nasty.

She yelled, "Hurry up, hurry up, come on girls!"

I did not want to listen to this after the whole week.

I looked at her and said, I probably shouldn't have done this, "You know, we're not students!"

"You're not?"

"No."

"Well I don't care who you are, hurry it up!" By the time I got to the till, she was beet red. Then she was all very sweet, you know, 'The hot water is over there.' And I thought, '*You treat people like crap, you hate your job, and everybody here hates their job.*' Every teacher I met in that school was so negative.

Out of the three art teachers, one character is all about process, eureka, very excited, embracing everything and very tactile.

The second character was very rigid, all about technique. One day the kids were doing a value drawing, and she told them, "Nobody start the eyes, I saw someone draw eyes and they weren't doing them right, so nobody is to draw eyes until I show you how to draw eyes." Two months on one drawing! They all hated it, and nobody wanted to be there.

The third character had this attitude, 'I don't know about art, I don't care about art, I just teach photo. And this is how the camera works, here is my worksheet from 35 years ago, come back in a week.' The kids were all over the place, just mayhem.

And the three art teachers were always arguing and talking about one another behind each other's back. Even in the lunchroom, the shop teacher complained about the murals somebody put up and how they looked like crap. It seemed as if everybody was so depressed.

There was nothing in the art rooms. Photography was terrible. There was one sink in the whole art room and it was shared by photo and art so there was paint and developer in the same sink. Nothing was labelled. There were open containers with fixer and the kids thought it was soap. It was unbelievable. Because there are three people and nobody is organized and there's no communication, and they're fighting over territory, and there's this health hazard left, right and centre. There wasn't much in terms of technology either. They had three computers at the back of the room that constantly didn't work. There was a printer which was only in the office so if the teacher wasn't there, the students couldn't work independently, and the printer regularly screwed up. I also found that there was this attitude with the teachers that 'we don't have technology so we can't do anything.' This is the excuse. This is why they never show images. We're in an image-based class and they never show images. How do you teach visual literacy without showing visuals? It was ridiculous! There wasn't even an overhead projector. Nothing. They didn't have anything.

Until today, I thought it was going to work, but the Teacher Education Office is pulling me out of there because there are a lot of problems with the placement. I kept saying no, I don't want to rock the boat, I'm fine, but I did feel pretty alone. It was traumatic and I've had three weeks to process it now. When we went for the debriefing with our cohort, I didn't really have anything to share, there were these papers where we jotted down ideas and I was using a brown pen, a brown marker, and when they held up the posters, I could just see that brown so clearly. All my comments were so negative and I don't know if anyone else noticed the connection between the colour of pen and comments that were being made, and not just negative, but also very jaded or cynical.

When I look back, there was a lot of racism from teachers towards students. It was a very diverse school. There were so many inappropriate comments, almost ageism, where the teachers thought that because they're older or wiser that they can treat everyone below them terribly. For example, during the first class I was standing at the front with this authority figure and the authority figure points to a kid in the front row and says, "You're going to know their name by the end of this class because they are going to drive you crazy." In front of the entire class, and that kid is just sitting there, wondering, '*What did I do?*'

I just sat down. I thought. '*I don't need this.*' What is the point? I want to know why there isn't a re-evaluation. How do those people keep their jobs? I just know I paid a lot of money and I worked pretty hard to get that money and I saved it up and I'm in a lot of debt and I didn't anticipate this kind of disorganization. I was just really disappointed and I feel relieved that I didn't internalize all the problems as my fault or that I can't be a teacher.

I've been selective in that I don't think I ever said the teacher's name. I was really surprised that I wasn't able to share it in the cohort, and that doesn't make sense to me, even now, I don't really get the bureaucracy of it. I understand that we don't want to get into this spiralling negative discussion but at the same time it was really real. It was real people in the situation at this moment. It's going to happen to others and how are they going to deal with that if they think that everything is always the way they have had it? So I don't understand why that isn't part of the process. Why aren't we able to talk about this freely? I know, Code 5, this is Code 5, but honestly, this is what happened to me and I'm not allowed to talk about it. Everyone has this fear about Code 5. No one wants to talk. I don't know what that person thinks so I'm not going to say anything. Sometimes there are moments where you think, Code 5, what? I just need to get this off my chest! It made me feel exactly how I had been feeling, that there's no support and no one seemed to really think that what I was experiencing was that big of an issue. And it was so much of a non-issue that I wasn't even able to talk about it, that's how I felt. It is dangerous because they want to keep people coming into the program, and once you're in it, they want you to stay in it. I became very aware of that over the two weeks, that it is an industry. I just felt like it was all about money. The teachers that I was working with on the short practicum were there because of money not because they cared, and then the program itself that I'm in, it's really costly, it's supposedly revered, and I felt really proud of myself for getting into the program. When I told people that I was in this program they were like, 'Wow, I'm so proud of you.' And then once I'm here, it's like okay, why was it so hard to get in, what is really happening here? I don't feel like everyone in our program is becoming a cookie-cutter image of a teacher. I don't feel like they are because there are so many diverse personalities and opinions, even now, after this long being in it. During the practicum, one of the girls dropped out because of health issues, and so this is now a fear that people are starting to drop like flies, and she was the third person to drop out.

As I think about it, I'm coming up with the word endurance. I just got to get through it. During the short practicum, I just kept referring to the light at the end of the tunnel: two weeks. I think through the whole experience, conversing with my family and hearing their side of it, I needed some validity. I needed someone to say, "You know what, you're a tough cookie and you can stick it out, but you don't need to. You don't need to do this. This isn't about your survival. This isn't what you signed up for. This isn't what anyone else is going through."

I felt like I was overreacting a little bit

I wasn't that assertive about the difficulties on practicum because I felt, and maybe this is my character and also just being female, that I didn't want to show emotion, not wanting to overreact, we get labelled with that, and especially me, I'm a pretty emotional person and that makes some people uncomfortable. There is a part of me that was really excited to just see all of my peers again, and getting back to the cohort community and feeling support, being able to talk and share stories that they had, and hear the good times or hear the crappy times they had. When we came back to debrief about a practicum, there wasn't a lot of freedom to talk about the practicum, so that was kind of hard because they were only encouraging positive stories. We heard lots of good stuff which in a sense made me feel better. There are other ways of this happening and I was so glad that not everyone had the kind of experience like I had. This is a learning experience and I'm learning exactly what I do not want to be in the classroom, if I decide to follow this through. Looking back, I felt like I was overreacting a little bit.

Sometimes I'm not sure that I want to become a teacher. I'm happy that I'm having this experience and I know it's beneficial to me, but I'm open to other avenues. After seeing a negative environment like the one on my practicum, I know I could never work in one for very long. The only reason I would stay is for the students. Even after just two weeks, I got cards from the kids! It felt like I made some connections with people in those classes whereas two months had gone by in the school year and the teachers did not know the names of their students. I know I'm not there to be anyone's friend, and I hope that that wasn't my intention when I was talking to those students, but I really felt like they taught me something.

I had those teaching moments, where I was at the front of the class and something hilarious would happen. The class was so diverse, some kids had been in Canada for six months and some have been here for two years and from all over the world, all different kinds of backgrounds, war-torn countries, and for some, it was their first time ever in a school, and language levels were pretty low. I was trying to do some activities, group work with people who don't speak the same language, and it was so interesting. It could have been frustrating and I think at times parts of it were, but it just became this wonderful, I don't know, it sounds airy-fairy, but just a connection between people beyond words. One example of this is I had these two kids playing *Pictionary* with clay.

One kid made this clay fork and the Ugandan boy is like, "I know what that is, but I don't know the English words."

"Well say that in your language." He did.

I turned to the Korean boy and said, "What is this in Korean?" And it was such a nice exchange. I hope it was positive for them.

Now I'm thinking about this one girl who missed the first three days of the first week because she got beat up. She said, "Oh, it is because I'm a lesbian and everybody hates me."

The teacher told me her attendance is a problem. She never shows up anyways. So I tried to remember students like her, and when they would come in, I would say, "Hi, how is it going? Nice to see that you came today. What are you going to work on today? If you need any help I'm around. If you have any questions about the darkroom ask me."

I spent one day working with her one-on-one, where I showed her how to develop film and the next day she was showing someone else how to do it, and with such pride. I thought that was neat. All she needed was one person to take the time out of their day to show her how to do it. She just needed to feel like she was valued in this room by someone who knew her name and saw her. I was just so excited by little things like that, and that's what made going to that school doable.

I guess we're all our biggest critics, but I can think of a couple of instances that have stayed with me and they stay for a reason. I hope that I use them in a way not to do it again. Just dealing with some behavioural problem students and how I spoke to them, or what I said to them. We did an activity in groups, and one girl said, "Why, why do we have to?"

And instead of me answering because I want you to get to know other people or I'd like you to interact with students you don't know, maybe you can mix and make connections, I said, "Because I asked you to."

I really wished I hadn't said that. I wasn't yelling. I said it like that, and I thought, '*Really, why am I all of a sudden this power figure? Why didn't my rationale come to the end of my tongue?*' Instead this power message came to the end of my tongue much quicker than my rationale. It really made me think about the authoritative figure at the front of the room, and just how our system is innately flawed. I don't agree with that kind of classroom but that is sort of how the system is set up. It's about evaluating grades and not progress, or mistakes, and so if I continue on in this field, I hope that I'm able to get my own class at least and bring some of my values and my idea of evaluation or criteria. I still really don't think of myself as a teacher but when I'm in that setting, I play the role and it kind of surprises me.

There was another situation where I was going around talking to students, and one kid had his head on the desk. I asked what was going on. He said he didn't feel well. His stomach hurt and he had a headache. I just kept asking him more questions.

"Did you have breakfast?"

"No."

"Are you sleeping?"

"Yeah."

"OK, what did you have for dinner last night?"

"Nothing."

"What did you have for lunch?"

"Nothing." He hadn't eaten in two days. I know adolescents can be kind of dramatic sometimes but if he says he hasn't eaten in two days, how is he sitting there?

I said, "You need to go get some food." But he didn't have any money. I offered to give him money but he said no, he could take care of himself.

"You know what, if you can then you better start! You need to eat." I mentioned it to my sponsor teacher and that's when he gave me the 'you are trying to save every student' crap.

I asked, "Is there some kind of aid or counsellor that should be alerted?"

The student also mentioned that he spent all day moving by himself, he lives by himself. Just to add another piece of information, he is from Korea, minimal English, so he's probably a satellite kid, lives here by himself, lives off instant food, and maybe we should get someone to look out for him. I felt like maybe I shouldn't get so involved or feel so emotional about the situation, maybe it's not my place, or maybe it is not as bad as it seems from my point of view, maybe it's not, but it seemed bad for him, and I'm honestly worried about him. So I would go home and I would think about all those people, all those kids.

It is just so interesting to see what kids are working on, what they're interested in, and what I can contribute. I'd bring stuff in, resources for them, and that was rewarding to me. It is just like collaboration, if that's the way school can be then I want to be there. Well even if there's just a slight, remote possibility for some children to be in an environment like that, this industry needs me. Education needs people like me because after two weeks the students were so responsive and engaged. My sponsor teacher was a very negative person, and he kind of mocked me a couple of times.

He said, "Oh yeah, I can tell you got that sparkle in your eye, still trying to learn their names, still trying to touch their souls," or something like that and it was really hurtful.

That wasn't my intention. I wasn't trying to save anyone. I was trying to survive the two weeks there, and in the process, I felt like there were other people needing someone to hang on to. I learned a lot of really great lessons from that even though it was tough.

I have to be a good role model

The short practicum was really about my transformation from a student in so many ways. My wardrobe became a teacher wardrobe, even now in my private time, I have different clothing; the private me versus my other identity as a teacher. I don't feel as comfortable. I feel a lot more formal. I feel like people view me differently. I looked at it as a role model, how when I'm in a classroom, I must be very aware of the eyes on me, and how I am in private, with friends. I'm really conscious of that appearance and I have to be a good role model. We're so used to seeing teachers just as teacher. When I was a student, and I saw my teachers outside of the school, those specific incidents stuck with me. I remember I had a math teacher named Bruno and he was always very strict. I didn't really like him, but then I went to swimming lessons and he was there wearing a lime green Speedo, and ever since that encounter I thought he was just a hilarious guy, like, oh my god he has a lime green Speedo! It changed how I viewed him as a person and as a teacher. He was really strict, but after I saw him in that bathing suit, I thought for sure he has a sense of humour!

When I was on the short practicum, I wondered, how much do I disclose or how much of my personality do I offer to students as a teacher? Because teachers, in my mind, should not divulge a lot about their personal lives or about their personal interests, their opinions, they should be neutral in those things. I feel such an inner passion or excitement when dealing with students, and I think that will lead to fulfillment as a teacher, and that feeling is the reward, a spiritual reward, from personal engagement on so many levels with different people of different backgrounds and different ages. It's strange how the school can easily be transferred into the private life, but the private life can't be so easily transferred into the school life.

When I'm in my student role, I'm a lot less sure of myself and a lot more self-centered. I focus on my studies and I'm always worried about how my work is going to be received by the expert, the professor, so I feel very aware of that relationship. But when I'm the teacher, it totally changes. I make a conscious effort to speak with confidence, not to say "um," even though I want to say 'um,' or 'maybe' or 'sometimes.' When I speak I feel like I'm not that sure of myself or I don't want to make too huge statements. I think it's linked to gender. I sometimes preface my knowledge with, "I don't really know."

So when I'm in the role of the teacher, I try to make that disappear because I'm aware that if I start that way, then automatically, how they receive me is going to change. If I go up there very confident, exuding those male qualities, then they will be a lot more receptive. It's very weird! It's very odd because the school is a very male environment, patriarchal, and you know, it's all top down and yet women are the main employees. I definitely feel very interested in female roles and female depictions or traits that are supposedly female, so I'm constantly looking at my own female identity, and how that relates to my environment. It is just about equal opportunity regardless of gender and so it's not just something that women can engage in, but that men can engage in too. I believe in equal chance, equal opportunity, I believe in community and I believe in inclusion.

As an artist, I'm a lot more experimental. I'm more comfortable with things not working out, a lot more comfortable with not finding answers to questions, as opposed to when I'm writing an essay for an academic class. As a student-teacher, I really want to find answers to my questions. As an artist, I feel like all those preliminary projects that are total failures or just crap, they lead you to something good. But the artist is invalid in the academy, in a written scholarly way; those kinds of failures aren't addressed or valued in the same way. I've been negotiating those things for some time now. One of the things that a lot of us have been feeling from this becoming art teachers is taking on the curriculum. It is so foreign, whereas we can write out a lesson pretty easily and feel inspired by it, but then we have to start using this language and categorizing everything and it just rules the life out of you. When I'm in that teacher role, I try to sound confident but I'm always aware that someone in the room might know more than me. And if they do, how am I going to have to change the lesson. From the teacher's point of view, you have to kind of gauge the way you are going to represent the material and what level you're going to present it at. For the sake of accessibility, you want to start at a basic level so that everyone is included. If someone raises their hand and lets you know that they are actually at a totally different place, they know more about the topic and have more insight and experience than you do, then on the spot, I have to be able to harness that.

I think it's really important to be aware of our limitations within ourselves but also with other people. Specifically when you're talking about certain subjects, we have no idea what's going on in a person's head. Some students may have had negative experiences in life, and traumatic memories may be triggered. For example, my mum is a teacher and she had a refugee from Bosnia and at that time, she was teaching Grade 5 and they were doing biology and she brought out the anatomy manikin that has all the organs that come out. She didn't even think about how this could affect kids, and he saw this and ran out of the room screaming. Right at that moment, she sat down and said, "I need to think about what this little boy has seen. I need to think about him and how he is constantly seeing things in a way that none of us can relate to."

I feel very close to that topic and I try to be aware of such possibilities with students. I think it is really important from a teacher's point of view, if you even slightly feel like this is not going over so well, no one is engaged, or this is boring or this is offending someone, then you have to follow that feeling and somehow address it or resolve the problem. Be aware of how we are embodying the role of teacher. Recognizing what we feel is a culturally appropriate way to respond to someone, even if it is just basic conversing, for example, making eye contact, the way we express our listening, that kind of thing, that's not the same for everybody, especially if they are from a different culture.

I really think because of the position we are studying to become there is the politics of the teacher and the teacher's relationship between the public and the government and it seems quite political. In the class that I'm in right now we are learning about where the money comes from and who says what goes, how being part of the union is not just your responsibility on the job, it is your responsibility off the job. We talk about all these court cases that they used to illustrate that point, where teachers are prosecuted because of their private life or activity in their private life. How some teachers have been let go because they breached the code of conduct as a teacher. It is interesting. It is a political profession, and you don't think of it that way as a student. Even right now, we haven't become teachers yet so really our only knowledge of teachers is from our own experience of being a student. Just thinking that teachers are bound by their job in that way, they may have to give up some of the liberties that they have in their private life. I guess it makes sense, but in other ways, well, that is a lot of freedom to give up. Teachers have a lot of power and so I think that teachers should use it wisely, to empower others. I think a classroom should be a safe space and a constructive and positive space, and everything is not always going to be easy but hopefully there is a positive outcome or lesson learned from all life experiences.

It feels good so far

I'm fairly ready for the long practicum. My new sponsor teacher seems really nice. She's really relaxed, which is good for me because I haven't been very relaxed, you know, some anxiety. I think we are going to team-teach for the first week, so I have been kind of working on my lesson plans and units and stuff, but she said don't worry about it until you get here. So that is perfect. It feels good so far. There is the teacher that I'm going to be working with and she has an artist in residence. Every time I've gone there, I leave feeling so excited and so relaxed. It seems like a really neat place to be. Even just from being there two or three times and observing their styles of clothing and hair, they just seem really neat. One of the ladies has bright pink hair! And the teachers at this new school seem to know all the names of students just from walking down the hall. It is a friendly rapport.

My sponsor teacher introduced me to every single person, she got me a library card, and this was all on the first day. I was just in shock!

At the end of the four-hour visit, I said to her, "Thank you so much!" And I was almost in tears, and I said, "Thank you so much for your hospitality, I can't wait to work with you."

When I'm at home for a little bit, or talking to other people in the cohort or friends in other cohorts, and they are all stressed out about lesson planning and stuff and I think, '*Oh maybe I should do some.*' I make my own stress. Sometimes there is an underlying rivalry, as if they are saying, "This is how much I've done, and how much have you done?"

We want to show our strengths, what we are good at, what we've accomplished. I think in the last week I've just been trying to relax and just think about how it could be such fun. Being a teacher could really be fun and I want to remember that. It could be such a creative and exciting job.

I think I will feel visible once I'm in a classroom. Right now I'm kind of behind the scenes preparing the stage, the long practicum. My family is aware of the phase that I'm in. I suppose our own experiences and identity affect the lens through which we experience everything, including this, so just who I am, my gender, my class, everything really affects me. It determines how I'm interpreting and taking in the information that I've got through this program, and how I relate to students on the practicum and students in my program. It affects everything.

A game of dramatic hats

I know I have progressed since I joined this program and I know I've learned things, but I don't feel amazingly prepared. I heard my sponsor teacher never signs up for student-teachers because the last three have not passed. Apparently, the students were not good placements, and that can happen, but three is a lot. When I sat down to look at everything, I felt totally overwhelmed. I spent two days writing one lesson. I was totally freaking out. I put so much pressure on myself for it to be perfect and I knew I was going to email it to the sponsor teacher, and I was worried she was going to think it was bad. In that moment I didn't think I could cope, it just became such a big, huge obstacle in my mind. I just had a breakdown and I wanted to quit.

I definitely think the long practicum was the hardest thing I ever had to do emotionally and mentally. I was struggling throughout the entire thing. Almost every day I wanted to quit. I didn't enjoy that part of it. Every morning I woke up and felt nauseous. I had lots of health issues and went to the doctor often. I probably went to the doctor at least five times and was constantly getting new prescriptions for sleeping pills, for ulcer preventative type medication. I wasn't eating and I wasn't sleeping and was constantly going to the bathroom and it was really uncomfortable. But all day I had to pretend like I was fine. It was just awful. I don't know if that is the stress of the practicum, the stress of that specific situation with the sponsor teacher I had, or if it is just the profession and my personality. I honestly didn't feel like I had enough stress coping tools within me. Physically and emotionally, I was just a mess.

Every single day I went home and cried. It was good if I could make it to my door. Sometimes I would make it to the bus stop and start crying, it was really really emotional and I think it was a combination of just the type of person I am and how I deal with stress and just that experience. I felt that my relationship with my sponsor teacher and faculty advisor was really superficial. I think that they have really made me question whether this is the right job for me.

The relationship with the sponsor teacher was really destructive. It wasn't caring and any time there was something positive, it was very odd. It was a very odd relationship. It moved back and forth between comfort and discomfort. At times I would think, *'Oh maybe it's okay, she doesn't mind sharing her classroom with me,'* and then there would always be an incident that made me realize, or reminded me that I'm in her space.

Even though she would say things like, "This isn't my room, this is your room now." A student would come up and ask her a question and she would play dumb and say, "Oh, I'm not your teacher anymore," knowing I didn't know the answer. So even when she had an opportunity to help me in those situations, she wouldn't.

Because of the nature of being a student-teacher, you are guided to believe you hold a certain amount of authority, that you have a certain amount of responsibility and that this is your classroom when you go on your long practicum. For everyone it is really different, depending on what your sponsor teacher is like. Some people really facilitate that role and other people make it a goal to deter that from happening. They will publicly rob you of that in front of students, or in front of other colleagues.

In my own experience, small comments, like a student asked a question for the homeroom teacher, and my sponsor teacher said, "Go ask your real teacher." Okay what does real teacher mean?

So the student turned to me to ask something and I don't know the answer, so then I have to ask the sponsor teacher again. It was very superficial, a game of dramatic hats. It was not real. It doesn't make sense. And why can't that person answer the question of the student? Especially one I wouldn't know the answer to. It was very theatrical. My sponsor teacher would take off her hat, and no longer be a teacher. It was really bizarre.

There would be times where I would be told in a dramatic sense, "This is your room. You create your rules. You organize the room how you want." And then a day later, there would be comments about how many pencils were missing, how her supplies were going missing and I needed to track those better and other comments too.

Finally, after a month, I was left alone. Until that point every single lesson was observed and written up as an observation. Every single one. Finally I asked if I could be left alone, and that day was amazing compared to the rest of the time because if I made a mistake, she couldn't see it. Thank goodness for that! It was between me and the students, and so at the end of the day, she came back to see how I did, or sometimes, she came back when I was out of the room.

Once she was there looking at the drawings the Grade 8's completed, and she said, "Boy they're sure shitty."

"Oh you think so, I thought they were all right. The students tried pretty hard."

"Yeah but look how fuzzy the lines are! Why are they so fuzzy? I was really confused by that and then I saw your demo drawing and realized they just copied the way you did it." She got meaner. It got to the point where she asked me, "Haven't you ever taken a drawing class?"

That was the tone of the long practicum.

I felt really abused. When I would get home, everyone would say, "You know what, this lady is a bitch. Let it run over you. Don't let it get to you. If anything this is a great experience on how to work under someone who is difficult."

Whenever I felt like I had reign over the room, she would remind me that I didn't and I'd have no confidence again. I had a lot of fear of her, almost terror. I was terrorized. I really felt like that. I was being pushed in all these directions, all the time. Every day I would have a list two pages long of all the things I had to remember to do. It was the only way I could start falling asleep, to write out everything in my head. Every night I would have nightmares. I wouldn't sleep, I would toss and turn, I would wake up after four hours of sleep, feel nauseous, I couldn't eat, and then I'd go to work. It was like that for two months. Even now, two months later, I get that nauseous feeling in my stomach when I drive by the bus stop I got off at to go to my practicum school.

I did six weeks at 80% and it ended so abruptly. On that final day, I remember I gave her a gift and a card. I left the room and came back and she said, "Well that card was very nice, thank you for that, okay so you're done here, you can go." I wasn't done. This is at 3 o'clock and she told me to leave.

I said to her, "I can't go yet, there's a lot of stuff I need to do. I want to finish the marking." It wouldn't be fair to the kids to have her mark stuff that she didn't even know about. I almost got kicked out.

She just kept saying, "No. No. You're done, don't worry about it, you did a great job, it's fabulous, I'm really satisfied. Just go." But I didn't buy it. She wanted me to leave. She had been waiting and waiting and waiting to get her room back. And I still think about that. It is still on my mind.

A number of times I likened the entire experience to being on a Reality-TV show. I had these people who gave me challenges and every week or every day, I had to be in front of them as judges. I felt like I was constantly being picked apart. I knew that all these people were watching me, and all these expectations are being put on me that weren't being modelled. There was a moment where my sponsor teacher got really frustrated because we weren't meeting regularly. I would give her my lesson plans sometimes the day before, sometimes three days before, and sometimes she read them and other times she didn't.

I said, "Do think we could have a meeting because I really need some guidance." We had a meeting and she wanted to point out all the things I wasn't doing right. At that point I was getting more confident and so I said, "Well actually I did do that, or I thought I was doing that, and if you look at this lesson plan ..." And that's when it started to become evident that we weren't working as a team.

She got very frustrated and it was the first time I saw a weakness in her. And she said something like, "Look, I really feel like I'm not doing my job, I don't know how I'm supposed to do this, and I'm really not comfortable with the way things are going."

If I hadn't had support, my family and my friends, I probably would have dropped out. Even they had some fears, and a couple of times they said to me, "Do you think you're going to pass this?"

"I don't know. I hope so." I just kept saying to them, "I'm doing my absolute 100% best, actually maybe even 110%."

I knew that I committed myself completely. I don't know how someone with their own family with children could have done this. I couldn't have. Even if I had been married and my spouse wasn't in the program, that would've been a huge stress. Most evenings I didn't get home until 6:30 p.m. and then there's always work to be done. I got home, I would lie on the couch for an hour, maybe eat something, work till midnight, go to sleep and be back to work at 7:45 a.m. the next morning.

On practicum you are led to believe you have this role of authority, it is slightly given to you and then it is taken away. I didn't realize to what extent we were so vulnerable. I don't feel very confident or comfortable in this role. So I still feel quite unsure about myself. In that sense I guess I realized who I was as a student-teacher after the fact, thinking that really it was a bit of a charade. So it will be interesting to see in the years to come how I feel about my teacher experiences. I just wonder if to teach art really kills it for me. I think in some ways there are some people who are artists, and some people who can juggle both those roles of teacher and artist, and I found it really hard to do. It was just so emotional in a way that my independent art practice isn't. As an artist I can be private and I don't have to be concerned about taking responsibility for other people. So that was something that came up and I'm still wondering if this is the right job for me. I think I will pursue teaching and if I realize after a year or two years it doesn't suit me then I can pursue other options, like working in galleries.

My challenge was to focus on the positive

I was really glad when the long practicum was done and I also felt it ended on a high note. One of my challenges was not to focus on the negative, and really focus on the positive. When I was in front of those two characters, the sponsor teacher and the faculty advisor, I had to present myself in a strong, confident, 'I'm in control' manner. In the end they felt proud of me because I had overcome the challenges that they thought I had, but I really felt that I had overcome different challenges. I know that in the end I learned so much. I think it was successful. I had a successful practicum, and I feel really proud of how hard I worked, and of the relationships that I had with the administration at the school and with the students at the school. This was the biggest thing I've ever done.

I felt even with the behavioural issue students, in those relationships, the standards were respectful, the relationships were very respectful. I feel like I did a lot of caring, and that my family and friends did a lot of caring for me. I did a lot of work with some of those students. There were a lot of students with poor home lives, behavioural issues, learning disabilities, chronic attendance problems, and they were never dealt with, they had never been addressed. Even if the work was causing me extreme amounts of stress and even if the students made me feel angry, I still cared about them as people. I really felt like I was putting so much energy into caring for these students and then I would go home and totally fall part.

For me, I would tell prospective students not to go into teaching right after an undergraduate degree. Take some time off, if you are a little bit older and you have life experience, you'll manage much better. If I didn't have those two things I would've dropped out. You should try to build your confidence before you come because you're going to get it dwindled a little. It's going to test you. It was testing my organizational skills, my ability to think ahead, to act on my feet, to mask my true emotions.

If I could do the long practicum again, I would take more time for myself. I would take better care of myself, eat, exercise, and sleep, and I would learn to meditate. I would try not to take it so personally.

One day the Physics teacher came into the classroom, his class was two down from mine. He was an older guy, maybe late 50s and you could tell that his job was his life. The kids really liked him. When you met him in the hallway, he would chat away to you. He was single, and he and I had a friendly relationship. He helped me a lot. Just in that minute way of being friendly to me, he was letting me know that he was looking out for me. I wrote him a card before I left because one day he came in and sat down and said, "What's up, Teach?" And he pulled up a chair and he said, "I can tell you are having a bad day, and you don't look well."

I just smiled and I knew I couldn't say anything. I said, "Thanks, thanks for talking the time to say hi." It was really meaningful to me. I felt like there were relationships like that that I created with the staff. It is a big job for a teacher to take on a student-teacher. I tried to be compassionate towards my sponsor teacher. A number of times I thanked her for allowing me to be in her space and for allowing me to use her resources and I really felt for her, especially because she was very unhappy in many aspects of her life, and she talked a lot about that with me.

What was interesting in my case was that at the exact same time as I was in my practicum, my mom had a student-teacher in her classroom, so it was very helpful to hear her feelings about what it is like to share a classroom. My mum said that as a sponsor teacher, you try not to let it get to you, but you wonder if the kids like the student-teacher better, and when you come back to class there is always two weeks where the kids accidentally call you by the student-teacher's name. She says it is not a big deal but you do notice those things.

I feel lucky to have my mother. She has mentored me in teaching. She helped me so much. On the weekends near the end of the practicum, I started going home every weekend and taking all of my school stuff with me, and she would sit down and say, "OK, what is your plan?" And I would go over my lesson plan with her. She would say, "OK, why are you doing it this way?" And that helped me overcome my gaps.

I also learned that I need to focus on limiting work, that personal time is as valuable. I had no personal time. I worked every moment on the practicum. I really had no personal life at all. I think that's partly what scares me about myself. I will allow myself to be consumed by work. I don't put boundaries up in the way that other people are really good at doing. I wasn't able to do that. I am wondering, if I try this for a year or two, will I just overwork myself? I don't want to totally burn out. I realized I really like smaller classrooms. I had my smallest class with 18 kids in ESL. I loved that class. It was so neat. They come from different countries where education is such a scary thing, there's physical abuse by teachers, and they had tremendous respect for me that was absent in my other classes.

It made us laugh at one point because I was talking to one boy from Sri Lanka, and I asked him, "Do you ever miss Sri Lanka?"

He said, "Oh I really miss it but I'm so glad I'm in school in Canada. I'm not good at writing and they always used to beat me. I was really afraid to make a mistake."

And I jokingly said, "Oh I'll never beat you!"

"Oh I know!"

And so we were laughing, and just little things like that. My experiences abroad, knowing what it feels like to be in a different place and speak a language that isn't mine, really made me comfortable around them. I felt like we fed off each other, they understood that I understood. Because we talked about that, we talked about what it was like to be in a different country, a different culture, with different foods, and all these changes and how they're doing and I commended them, "You're doing such a great thing right now."

It was really, really fun. That was the class where I was the most myself. I didn't feel like there were power struggles, as in some of my other classes. I had those kinds of challenges with students who were unmotivated. I didn't know what to do at first, and I'm not sure I have resolved how deal with it. I still think about some of those kids. It is hard because you see students who have been abandoned in some way or form. They're struggling. They don't believe in themselves and think they're not worth anything. It killed me to see people like that. It depends on who you are and what chance you've been given. I don't think they can be whipped into shape, they need help. There is a reason that they are doing what they're doing. Then there are times when you see kids that you know are going to be in trouble. I had one girl and she had no sense of right or wrong, no remorse. She was a big problem. She was asked not to come to school. She was so disrespectful and dishonest. And I wondered about her. What was her home life like? Where was she taught that she was a pain in the ass all the time?

I was going through my pictures from the long practicum, I took a lot of pictures, and I saw a picture of her and I thought, oh that girl is headed in the wrong direction.

I learned too that you can't please everybody. There was one student in particular, it was a real struggle with her, every time I would present what we were going to work on, it was like I was making her do the worst thing in the entire world. I didn't know how to deal with it. I was very frustrated.

I asked my mom what do I do and she said, "Make light of it." She said, "I have a kid like that and now whenever I introduce something I say, before we start, let's all agree that so-and-so is going to hate this and then they start realizing that they are so negative about everything, and now that kid laughs too."

I didn't have enough time with the student. One thing I did do was to give her special treatment, a job to do. She wasn't into the projects and she just whipped through it as she would everything and just did it half-assed.

So I said, "I really need your help," and gave her a job. She was happy to do it and I thanked her so much for her great work. We finally had a positive encounter together. I was tired of having the negative struggle.

Also, there wasn't a lot of technology in the school that was accessible to me. They had an opaque projector. It's huge. It is probably double the size of a monitor, and it's got a little conveyor belt with a crank and you put your piece of paper in, crank it through and it projects your paper onto the wall. Very archaic! The kids didn't even know what it was. So we used that quite often, for drawing, and it was kind of fun. It took a lot of time though so it wasn't that practical. The overhead projector was instrumental. I made two PowerPoint presentations and the kids thought that was neat to have a change. At the end of the practicum my sponsor teacher got a laptop, so it was nice to have a computer there because when someone was done they could go in, type up their artist statements and then they could type up artist statements for other kids.

I borrowed a DVD camera for the mural project. One of my challenges was to do a collective project with 30 kids. They all had different needs, and they didn't want to cooperate, so to make that work, I developed subprojects, so that two kids were making a DVD of the process, and they got to film and interview other kids and so on.

There were a lot of good things that I learned from my sponsor teacher, from observation, what kinds of images she used, how she dealt with different issues, and what she collects from galleries, and she has a box of materials and just pulls out items and away she goes. She spreads them out on the table and has everyone come over to look. So that was good. I wouldn't have thought of that.

There were so many unknowns before I went on the practicum. I wasn't aware of how many roles there were, how much energy it took and how I would adapt myself to those roles. It is interesting because there are a lot of roles that they don't even talk about before you go. We have a class now about these things. I wasn't even familiar with what techniques were out there, or how I would adapt myself into the disciplinary role. I hadn't thought about any of that. What do you do when the kid says, "I'm not doing it." Or just walks out? I had to confiscate a knife from one kid. I wasn't prepared for that. I didn't feel I had been trained for those incidents.

Becoming a good teacher

For a while I was quite negative, but recently I had to write a reflection for a class about what I think makes a good teacher, and if the university prepared me to become that teacher. It was a seven to eight page paper, and it felt good to lay out my positives and negatives a little bit more. I think I was pretty jaded or just feeling bitter or something, and in the end I thought, maybe I'm asking too much. I've outlined the things I think a good teacher embodies, and I also concluded that maybe it's not the role of university, maybe the university does not make you a good teacher, they just give you some development, that they probably hope you are already at a certain point before you come to them. So that was a nice realization because I put less on the university and more on me. I felt a lot more responsible, rather than they didn't do this, they didn't do that, and I feel I've done a lot of that this year. I feel pretty good taking ownership of my experiences.

I know I have a foundation as a good teacher. I came up with five things that I would like to work on as a teacher and I think I will keep building on them. A good teacher is someone who is caring, and caring I think is one of the most important ones. Someone who is reflective and someone who, and this one was kind of tricky, has awareness of school dynamics. I think it is so important, just being aware of the students' lives on a daily basis, body language, comments, silences. All these things, we have to be aware of because sometimes no one else is looking for it. I found that a lot in the school I was in, these kids were burning the candle at both ends and no one seemed to care and they just got whisked away at the end of the hour, to a new room and no one noticed them. No one said hello to them.

I've been thinking about adding to the qualities of a good teacher. This may be controversial, but somehow creating a spiritual classroom. When I say spiritual I don't mean religious at all, but modeling with awareness and respect and empathy to others, not just other people, but life forms. I don't know how to do that, maybe it is a very odd thing, but incorporating gardening for example. I think plants have a huge potential for power. I read this article recently that suggested if you can create a spiritual classroom then it deters students from being negative or harmful, or violent to others and to themselves, and it boosts that community, it creates a positive citizen. So that is the starting point, the beginnings of me being able to talk about it, and I think with time and thought and reflection, I will be able to articulate this better. It will change. Writing the reflection has been a good opportunity to think about that. Family members and friends are just so excited for me, a lot more than I feel for myself. Because they saw me go through that process and they were a support network for me in the down times, they are exhaling as much as I am exhaling, which is kind of interesting. There were a lot of times where I wanted to quit, and there were people who wouldn't let me, and I'm really grateful that they didn't. It's been an opportunity to discover myself and to make connections with others in ways I didn't expect.

I think I'm a little more sure that I would like to try it as a profession. Just because I'm in the program, I haven't accepted that this is going to be my choice of career. I think I should try to TOC, get a contract for at least two years and see how that goes and if it still doesn't feel quite right then maybe I will pursue something else. I think that from what I saw there seemed to be a lack of something in the schools and I would really like to try and fill that void a little bit if I can. It might take too much out of me, I don't know. It's strange. I don't feel like this process of becoming is done. There is a whole other thing now that I have to prepare for, that I actually don't feel prepared for: TOC'ing.

On Thursday, the very last day of school, it was sad. I didn't want to leave. The class finished at noon and I went into the old cohort room and there were seven people in there, just hanging out. We just sat and chatted. It was pretty telling. No one wanted to go. We stayed until about 3:30-4 p.m., and so it was sad. I mean, I wasn't overly emotional but something inside was kind of sad. That night everyone went out. It was just strange leaving the classroom and later that night, going out to a bar and having great fun, people taking pictures and acting like fools and dancing and letting it all out.

People hugged and said, "If I don't see you again, goodbye!" That kind of thing. It was quite sad. There are a lot of connections that you don't realize until that last day, what a huge thing you have shared with those people. Even with people I didn't necessarily like. People who drove me crazy all year, on the last day it was like, "Well take care!" "Good luck." "It was great." So that was nice.

Coming back into university, I got a new community, a new network. In the art teacher cohort I found great allies, and inspiration, and friends and mentors, and all kinds of great people that really helped me feel good about myself and validated my work. It wasn't just about wanting to be an art teacher, for me it was a lot bigger than that. It really helped me feel comfortable with myself as an artist and as a teacher. It really did reinforce those roles on me in a new way. For a long time before the teaching program, I didn't think I was an artist. I was very embarrassed when friends or family would say, "Oh she's an artist." And I would think, '*Oh no I'm not, I haven't done anything or I'm not good at producing work for myself.*' Going from art student to artist was really difficult for me. I was comfortable being an art student and once school ended then I became an artist supposedly, but what makes you an artist? So I was really uncomfortable with that. And now I feel much more comfortable with myself and a lot more confident in what I do, based on my knowledge and my practice. If I do something at home, doodling or some kind of small collage, or sewing or whatever, that's valid and I think I really undervalued it before taking this program. Now that I'm done, I feel contentment with myself, just satisfied. Regardless of how up-and-down it was, I'm going to get that piece of paper that is going to give me access to the profession.

You know, I just acquired some photos that are very interesting to me. I think that they will really help me inform that role of teacher because it is two albums. The first album is of my grandmother's history of being a teacher. It is her class photos from her career, and her staff photos. She wrote all the kids' names on them and it is so interesting, they were going to be thrown away. No one wanted them. I couldn't believe it because my mother has these same kind of class photos, my grandmother had them, and now I will eventually have them. And what about mine, how will mine add to the collection? And how can I use this collection, how can I reform it or recreate it or build on it? The second album is her retirement party. It took place in a gymnasium in the 1970s. This is a story. I've got this build up, then this conclusion and it's all in photo. I think there may be a few letters from my grandfather to my grandmother, because they lived in different places, and a lot of the time it is about teaching or logging. It is really exciting. I just got them yesterday, almost to the day that I finished the teacher education program.

AFTERWORD

WIDENING CIRCLES OF LIFE WRITING AS A LITERATURE OF SELF IN RELATION: A LETTER IN LIEU OF AN AFTERWORD

Erika Hasebe-Ludt
University of Lethbridge

We tell ourselves stories in order to live.

—Joan Didion

I live my life in widening circles
that reach out across the world.

—Rainer Maria Rilke

Writing is a transgression of boundaries, an exploration of new boundaries. It involves making public the events of our lives, wriggling free of the constraints of purely private and individual experiences. From a space of modest insignificance, we enter a space in which we can take ourselves seriously.

—Frigga Haug

Dear Anita, Ruth, Anne, and Nathalie:

As I sank into the folds of your stories of becoming teachers, I remembered my own. It has been close to 25 years since I entered the classroom that became the place where my teacher education unfolded and where my life as a teacher began. Yet, I remember as if it were just yesterday the tensioned spirit that filled the room between the excited expectations of new knowledge and new skills and the fear of not knowing, of self-doubt that this was the right choice I had made. And I remember the beginning of tentative connections and conversations with others who had heard the call of teaching. These were life-changing moments, and like your stories attest, Ruth, Ann, and Nathalie, they provoked lifelong questions and queries about what it means to be and become a teacher.

As the title of Joan Didion's collection of nonfiction essays and stories reminds me, "we tell ourselves stories in order to live." Your evocatively titled stories also remind me that we tell ourselves stories in order to teach. Through careful and caring collaborative inquiry, guided by Anita's attentive, appreciative listening, transcribing, and composing, the events of your lives as teachers became artfully rendered narratives that point to the power of an original literature of self in relation. Your lived experiences inside and outside the classrooms you entered became personal and public testimonies to your passions, beliefs, and values. As luminous exemplars of life writing, your stories speak to the significant potential of documenting and crafting such lived experiences in the first-person voice. This is the kind of storied material that has the emancipatory effect of, in Frigga Haug's words, "taking ourselves seriously" as women, teachers, and writers.

By braiding different ways of articulating and interpreting your unfolding sense of your own identity and world in relation to other worlds – those of your students, peers, teachers, administrators, family, foes, and loved ones – you remind me of the expansiveness of life writing in-between fiction and nonfiction. "There is no way to bring autobiography to heel as a literary genre," James Olney (1980, p. 4) points out. And regardless of the genre a writer proclaims to work in, as Hélène Cixous reminds me, "What is most true is poetic. What is most true is naked life" (1997, p. 3). It takes courage to write truthfully, especially in this profession that, with its rigid, prescriptive structure "just rules the life out of you," as Nathalie so poignantly wrote. It takes strength of mind and heart and body to undo a curriculum that has been inscribed with layers of racial and cultural politics, gendered and economic inequities, and discrimination against the most vulnerable and marginalized students in our communities. You astutely described the increasing climate of fear mongering and institutional bureaucracies that dominate our professional and personal lives.

And yet, through your storied meaning making, you were able to "sneak out of the cage," as Ann put it. You worked hard, practiced your craft, even when you faced failure, when you had to "walk around the mountain quite a few times," in Ruth's words. You kept walking, and you wrote yourself into a heart of wisdom with each and every small step. So I applaud your dedication and courage to reveal your struggles and tell your difficult truths, as young women, teachers, artists, and researchers. There is an inspiriting sense of hope unfolding from your visceral and intimate narratives of becoming teachers, rendered though literary and artful engagement with the world of teaching. You became visible to yourselves and to your readers, and you wrote yourselves into new dynamic identities, creating new pedagogical worlds with passion and care. So linger in your stories as places where the call of teaching has become, as Ted Aoki (2000) wrote, a world where one truly belongs together with others. I hope this letter finds you well and working in places of teaching and learning that inspire you and where you can inspire others.

Anita, Ruth, Ann, and Nathalie, thank you for the abundant gifts of your stories, and for letting me, as your reader and one of your relations, move freely into the folds of your luminous life writing in between my own stories. May your life as teachers and artists and writers continue to unfold in widening circles that reach out across the world. May you persevere in your pedagogical work of making and remaking a curriculum that is personal and political, and infused with your precious sense of responsibility to the word and the world.

With gratitude,

Erika

REFERENCES

Aoki, T. T. (2000). On being and becoming a teacher in Alberta. In J. M. Iseke-Barnes & N. N. Wane (Eds.), *Equity in schools and society* (pp. 61-71). Toronto: Canadian Scholars' Press.

Cixous, H., & Calle-Gruber, M. (1997). *Hélène Cixous rootprints: Memory and life writing*. New York: Routledge.

Didion, J. (2006). *We tell ourselves stories in order to live: Collected nonfiction.* New York: Alfred A. Knopf.

Haug, F. et al. (1987). *Female sexualization: A collective work of memory* (E. Carter, Trans.). London, UK: Verso.

Macy, J., & Barrows, A. (1996). *A year with Rilke: Daily readings from the best of Rainer Maria Rilke*. New York: HarperCollins.

Only, J. (Ed.). (1980). *Autobiography: Essays theoretical and critical.* Princeton, NJ: Princeton University Press.

BIOGRAPHY

Anita Sinner is an assistant professor in the Department of Art Education, Faculty of Fine Arts at Concordia University in Montreal, Canada. Her research areas include arts research, curriculum studies, life writing, social and cultural issues in education and interdisciplinary qualitative approaches. She has co-edited several books: *A Heart of Wisdom: Life Writing as Empathetic Inquiry* (Chambers, Hasebe-Ludt, Leggo & Sinner, Eds., 2012, Peter Lang); *Living Artfully* (Sinner & Lowther, Eds., 2012, Key) and *Writing the West Coast: In Love with Place* (Lowther & Sinner, Eds., 2008, Ronsdale).

Lightning Source UK Ltd.
Milton Keynes UK
UKOW03f1833160813

215479UK00001B/4/P